To the perfect little girl whose life was far too short.
You made me a mummy and helped shape me into the woman and mother I am today.

I publish this on what would be your 16th birthday, to put into print both the joy and the sadness, in the hope that sharing my experiences may help someone earlier in their journey.

My main hope is to be for others, the voice that I so desperately needed to hear in the early days of my grief and to normalize and talk about every part of my journey, without filter, enabling others to realize that however alone they may feel, they are not.

I hope that in publishing my journey I am doing my tiny bit to raise awareness of baby loss, miscarriage and infertility and in breaking down those taboos.

My beautiful girl,
I loved you for the whole of your life, and I will miss you for the whole of mine.
I hope above anything else that I have been and will continue to be the best mummy that I can to you.

Forever my baby girl
25th May 2005

ACKNOWLEDGMENTS

To all of my children, you each in your own way, at some point in your lives have made me fight for you and made me stronger.

For all the ways in which you have shaped me into the mother, and the woman I am today.

For all the happiness you bring me, both individually and collectively.

I am grateful for every single moment I get to spend with you (even the hard ones where all I want to do is scream and swear!)

Thankyou for being you, and in turn for making me me.

I can't wait to see what the future holds for you all.

i

PROLOGUE

This book is an adaptation of a blog I started several years ago, documenting experiences I went through, and the way in which they changed me as a person. But also following the journey, both physical and mental that I have been on for the past 16 years, the journey through pregnancy complications, baby loss, infertility and miscarriage to finally complete my family.

The journey as I navigate through motherhood and all of the obstacles I have had to overcome.

The journey that shaped me into the person and mother I am today.

It is not a magical tale of perfect births and fairy tale motherhood, in fact it couldn't be further from that, but it's MY story, MY journey, MY experiences, MY feelings.... things I never thought all those years ago that I would ever be confident enough to share with anybody.

The main goal of my writing was originally to just get stuff out of my head and onto paper, but as more and more people began to read my inane ramblings, the goals of raising awareness, of normalising loss came along.

Now I am confident enough to share, to put myself out there, and share some of the most private moments, in the hope that someone may find hope in reading it.

If even one person feels less alone on their journey, then it will have all have been worth it, I will have achieved something and found something positive to come out of my darkest moments.

ONE

So here goes...

16 Years ago, I was a person completely unrecognisable to the one I am today, the main reason for that being that 16 years ago I became a mother....

I would like to say I changed instantly from the moment I first realised I was pregnant – but in truth... probably not.

You see, my first pregnancy was not planned – though that is not to say it wasn't wanted – because from that very first moment – despite the enormous fear – I was only 18 and at university – from that very first moment, sat alone in the university toilets staring at the positive test, I knew I loved my baby, and I knew my life was about to change for the better.

That said, I, as a person, did not change from that moment – yes, I suddenly became increasingly aware of my maternal instinct, yes, I grew up very quickly – though I'd always been older than my years – but I was still the shy, quiet, shell of a person with no real fight in me, scared of my own shadow and afraid to voice my opinion.

That was all about to change.

I suffered terribly from sickness for the first 3 months, so badly I was unable to leave the house, and it is safe to say I wasn't exactly enjoying my pregnancy, though I was enjoying making plans for my new life as a mum.

My mum came with me to my midwife appointments, as I was far too scared and shy to go alone, she held my hand while I had my blood taken, as I shook with fear, felt sick with nerves, with no confidence at all.

I was a quiet, shy, embarrassed 18-year-old with no idea what I was about to experience.

I had done my research and decided to carry on at university, sitting my exams at 7 months pregnant and then planned on sending my baby to full time nursery, whilst I studied full time from the September when my baby would be only 2 months old.

At the time I thought that was the kind of parent I wanted to be, that was what I thought was expected of me....and at that time I was definitely one to conform to what I thought society believed was the right thing to do.

I remember the day things changed very well.

It was Wednesday 4th May 2005, and I was 30 weeks pregnant.

A routine midwife appointment 2 days earlier had shown my bump was measuring big for dates, I had been referred for an ultrasound. In my naïve 19-year-old head I was excited.... This meant I'd get to see my baby again; it might even mean it would be born a bit earlier than id expected... I couldn't wait!

I had gone to the hospital on my own, baby's dad was at work, and my mum had gone on holiday that morning. I remember sitting in the hospital waiting room feeling happy, feeling my baby kick, and being so excited to see the ultrasound screen again.... that feeling was very short-lived. In fact, that feeling has never once returned to me in the past 16 years.

What happened in that room changed my life and will stay with me forever.

I lay down on the couch as the sonographer put on the cold gel and started to run the scanner over my enormous belly. She didn't say a word, and I couldn't see the screen, but I was still so excited.

After a couple of minutes had passed silently, she asked me who I had come to the hospital with... when I replied that I was alone she asked me to get up carefully and explained that she was taking me upstairs to delivery suite to see a doctor and that I should phone somebody to come and meet me urgently.

The exact conversation is a bit of a blur, but I remember clearly her telling me that she had seen fluid in my babies' lungs and around its brain, that it was unlikely to survive.

I can still remember her walking me down the corridor through the maternity building, and into a staff lift, arriving onto delivery suite and her showing me into a room and telling me a doctor would be in to see me soon.

I was left alone in that room, my head racing with thoughts, having no idea what was going on for what seemed like forever, until my sister (also pregnant at the time), baby's dad, and my nanna arrived to be with me.

The doctor came and went and told me nothing except that my baby was extremely sick and that I'd be kept in hospital overnight until I could be transferred to another, more specialist hospital the next day.

I spent my very first night in hospital as an adult that night, an exceptionally long, sleepless night, with many tears and so much confusion.

At that point, I was still so scared of hospitals and doctors, I'd never been alone in the hospital before, never been to the doctors on my own, never been left with strangers looking after me.

I was absolutely petrified.

TWO

The next day was the day something inside me changed, the day I suddenly realised what being a mother really meant.

The day I learnt I would have to fight for my baby, that I would have to do everything in my power to keep them safe.

I arrived at the next hospital by ambulance, accompanied by my midwife and baby's dad. I had never been in an ambulance before and was terrified.

I remember pulling up in the ambulance bay and the driver opening the doors, as I stepped outside into the hot sunshine I was met by my mum (who had flown straight back from holiday). She was stood there with her suitcase, in her summer dress having come straight from the airport to be with me.

I can still remember the tears, and how relieved I was to have her by my side. I felt like a small child who just needed her mummy.

I remember walking inside the strange hospital, where I'd never been before, and being seated in a small waiting room amongst a sea of happy faces, of women and their partners happily waiting for their ultrasounds, coming out with huge smiles and little pictures, bursting with excitement. That had been me only 24 hours before.... Now that excitement had been replaced by fear, I felt sick as I waited to go into the ultrasound room once more...

I cried many tears that day.

After waiting for what seemed like forever, I was taken into a room and scanned by a lovely doctor – one who would soon become a regular fixture in my life.

After explaining that my baby was incredibly poorly, they had a condition called hydrops fetalis, she offered me the option of a medical termination, and sent us to a quiet room to think about it.

It was in that exact moment that I became a mother, there was no thinking done in that room, despite the midwifes (rather strong) advice to have a termination, I knew that was not even an option for me, there were many tears shed, and I was incredibly scared, but above all I was determined, determined to do everything I possibly could to give my baby the best chance.

In that moment I made the decision to become a stronger person, a mother who could fight for her baby.

Gone was the young girl who was so scared of hospitals and doctors and needles that she needed her mum to hold her hand – she was replaced by a mother – a mother who went back into the ultrasound room and told the consultant that no, I would not like a termination.

I wanted to fight for my baby, I wanted to do everything possible to give them the best chance of survival.

The consultant was supportive.

Amazing in fact.

She explained every single option we had and gave us her absolute best care and advice.

Straight away I underwent the first of countless medical procedures.

There were what seemed like endless tests, amnio reductions – (this is where a large needle was inserted into my uterus and several litres of fluid were drained into jugs), needle drainage – (where the needle was inserted through my stomach into baby's lungs and fluid was removed from there too), genetic tests, tests for infections, every test possible to try and find a cause, and every procedure they could attempt to try and save my baby.

Many of these were extremely painful, I can still vividly remember lying there in the ultrasound room watching the screen as the needle was inserted into my stomach and watching litres and litres of fluid draining out – the pain was immense, the lying completely still whilst so hugely pregnant was just as hard, but I was determined to endure whatever the doctors could throw at me.

All these things I went through out of love, from a love that hadn't been felt until that moment, in that small room, when fighting became my only option.

The next 4 weeks are all a bit of a blur to be honest, there were countless hospital appointments and procedures, a great deal of pain, and an almost infinite number of tears and prayers – but what I do remember clearly is the love that I felt, and the determination I had to do everything I possibly could for my baby.

Wednesday 25th May came around quickly, it had been decided that my baby needed to be born early to have a greater chance of survival and that a planned caesarean would give the best chance of that. It also meant that all the specialists, neonatal team and consultants that were necessary would be present for the birth.

I was 34 weeks and 5 days pregnant.

Shortly before the operation I was scanned, and had fluid drained from babies' lungs via a needle, for the last time, to try and get the lungs to expand prior to delivery and improve the chances of survival.

It was then that I felt the beginnings of labour, those first contractions, brought on by the procedure I had just endured.

Within 30 minutes I was taken to theatre.

There were a lot of people in the operating theatre, when my baby was born – more than I can either count or remember.

There were doctors, midwifes, students, paediatricians, it seemed the whole hospital wanted to see my baby born.

In that moment there was silence in the room, it seemed everybody was holding their breath, waiting…

Waiting…. but nothing.

Not a sound came from her.

It was a few minutes before they even told me that she was a girl, she had already been whisked into the resus room next door, and I hadn't even seen her.

I told my mum her name and then tried my best to listen to the doctors in the room next door with her whilst I was stitched up.

That was probably the longest half an hour of my life….

It was only once I was in the recovery room across the corridor that the consultant paediatrician came to speak to us.

He told me that they'd tried everything they could to help her, they had drained fluid from around her heart, and given her adrenalin but she was just too poorly – she was too swollen to get the ventilator into her airway.

He asked if I would like to see her before they stopped working on her.

Of course, I did. She was my baby, why wouldn't I?

I don't think I even breathed in those few moments it took for him to go back and get her.

He quickly walked back in and handed me my beautiful baby girl wrapped up in a towel, she was perfect.

She weighed 8lbs 13oz but she was tiny, her weight being due to her being so swollen and full of fluid.

She had the most beautiful strawberry blonde hair and the chubbiest little cheeks. I remember her nappy seeming way too big.

She had both fluid and blood still dripping out from her chest where the doctors had been draining it just seconds earlier.

I kissed her precious little face, breathed in her newborn smell and told her I loved her.

As I held her for that very first time, she very quickly slipped away.

It was only a couple of minutes before the doctor came back with his stethoscope and confirmed that my beautiful girls' heart had stopped.... she was gone.

A part of me died in that moment.

As I held my beautiful girl, the realisation that although I had just become a mother, that I would have no baby to take home, that I would never see my daughter grow up, that she would never call me mummy.... my worst nightmare had just begun.

Until that point, I hadn't believed that my baby would die, even though I'd been warned how poorly she was, even though I'd been told her chances of survival were small I'd never even contemplated that she wouldn't survive.

She was my baby. I was her mummy. That's just not how it works.

I knew nothing about baby loss at that time, I was 19 and had led a very sheltered life, I had never even heard of it happening – at least not in our privileged society, this was something that happened in poor countries, to other people, surely this wasn't real?

I had no clue at all.

THREE

I'm not sure how I got through those first few days.

I still can't think about it very much.

I still have regrets; still wish I'd done things differently.

But hindsight is a funny old thing.

I spent 4 nights in the hospital recovering from my caesarean, I was lucky in that I got to spend a lot of time with my beautiful baby, that all her family came to see and hold my precious girl and the hospital created some precious memories.

I was lucky that my sister – after being told that it had a baby girl (before knowing that she had not survived) had been and bought some tiny clothes for her – and I'll never forget her helping me to dress my baby in her own clothes. I should add that she also bought a balloon and card etc…but whilst she was out shopping, she was told she had died, so the balloon was discarded as far as I'm aware in the public toilets… I don't even dare to think how she must have felt in that moment – she too was pregnant, due only 6 weeks after me, it must've been horrendous.

I was lucky in that whilst I was still in the hospital my mum visited the funeral directors and sorted out funeral arrangements for me – something I had no idea about, something I couldn't even contemplate.

Lucky that she also went and bought a beautiful white butterfly dress for her to be buried in, and the tiniest little bracelet, those things that I couldn't do myself, but that have created some of the only memories I have.

There are also some not so nice memories too.... Some that still haunt me now 16 years down the line, some that have shaped the way I live my life, but above all I was 19, and a mother, with no baby to take home.

Things were hugely different then to what they are now 16 years later – I know now that most hospitals have specialist bereavement suites, cold cots and a huge amount of support.

That wasn't my experience at all.

I was left in a room at the end of a corridor on delivery suite – put there I'm sure because it was the best place they had – I cannot fault the staff at all – the midwife who looked after me in theatre and after her birth was the loveliest, most caring woman and I will remember her, and be thankful for her forever.

She took such good care of my baby, and of me.

Unfortunately, being on delivery suite meant that I was subjected to endless newborn cries, labouring women, and every time I left my room for the bathroom, saw happy excited families carrying balloons and gifts coming to see new lives just being born.

It hurt.

A lot.

I do remember my auntie and uncle coming to visit me, they came bearing pink gerberas – (still my favourite flower to this day) and a beautiful shawl my auntie had made for my baby. We sat and made small talk - then heard a woman labouring down the corridor - this sound had been haunting me throughout the night as I tried to ignore everyone else's happiness....

But I will never forget how much my uncle made me laugh as he copied her – it hurt so much I was holding onto my stitches - but it was the first time I had smiled in days.

I'll never forget that.

Or the friend who came to visit and asked if she could see and hold my baby. I felt honoured to share her with someone. So happy that she got to meet my baby.

There were nice memories amongst the sadness.

Memories of her tiny pink clothes and trying on her beautiful white dress. Those memories will be forever etched into my heart, and these days, those are the memories I can look back on and smile.

I'm not sure if cold cots were even a thing back then, id certainly never heard of them until a few years later. But there wasn't one.

This meant that my baby was taken away from me at night, and as one midwife put it "ill just take her back to the fridge now."

I was 19 and naïve, id never experienced death before, I didn't know what to expect, but I did know that I didn't want my baby taken away from me, and I also know that I was shocked and surprised when she was brought back to me and she was cold. I ached for the warm newborn I had held just hours earlier, I cried at how her little body had changed.

But she was still perfect.

Still my beautiful baby girl.

I vividly remember one day, a couple of days after she had been born, the midwife wanting to take her back from me and I didn't want to let her go. I pretended to be asleep with her in my arms, knowing they wouldn't wake me or try to remove her whilst I slept. I lay there for what felt like forever, but was probably only half an hour, whilst the midwife kept asking my partner if I was ready for them to take her.

He told them not until I woke up.

Eventually she reappeared with a fan to keep her cold.

I was freezing and wrapped us both in the shawl my auntie had made for her and just lay for as long as I could before finally admitting defeat and saying goodbye.

To this day I will not own a fan.

I hate that memory.

I hate that that was the only way I could hold my baby.

I am so happy that things have changed now. That parents now, overall, can have access to a cold cot and spend as much time as they want with their babies.

I am happy that generally, there is access to bereavement suites and parents no longer had be surrounded by other parents and newborns. That they can now be somewhat sheltered, even if only for a short while. That they can be allowed to grieve in peace.

I was visited by a bereavement midwife whilst in the hospital and they did take some lovely hand and footprints of my baby, and a lock of her beautiful hair for me to keep. They also gave us some clothes and a blanket, along with many leaflets signposting us to support.

They meant well. But the support was virtually non-existent.

I know that this has changed dramatically over the past few years. I support and follow many charities who supply memory boxes, who do plaster castings of babies' hands and feet, who supply sets of clothing and who take photographs. The support is much greater now – and although mainly through charities set up by bereaved parents – it is there, and it is easily accessible.

I am so happy to see all of this.

I am not bitter.

Maybe I was once, but now I am only glad, glad that others going through such unimaginable pain can seek comfort and support in ways that I couldn't.

FOUR

Getting into the car 4 days after having my baby and leaving the hospital without her is possibly the hardest thing I have ever done.

I remember walking out of the ward, into the lift, and out into the fresh air. To the same ambulance bay that id arrived there in only 3 weeks earlier, seeing the same happy faces, watching others carry their newborns out into the big wide world for the first time.

I don't know how I got into the car, or how I even breathed without her that day. But I remember the physical pain from my caesarean as we went over the speed bumps on the long journey home. Maybe the physical pain masked how I was feeling emotionally, who knows.

Back home I threw myself into making a scrapbook, choosing music for her funeral, and hiding from the world.

I sat for hour after hour listening to songs trying to find the right one for my baby, I received what seemed like an endless stream of sympathy cards and flowers, and I spent what seemed like days deliberating over what to write on the card for my baby's funeral flowers…

I remember the vicar coming round and sitting across the dining table as he asked what songs and prayers I would like at her funeral – I remember thinking – how the fuck do I know?!

I'm not exactly an expert, this was not how it's supposed to be, this is not what I planned.... I remember wanting to scream at him, at everybody....

Instead, I just sat quietly, let my mum and the vicar choose something they thought was suitable– I wasn't ready for this, I couldn't do it. How was I supposed to make that kind of decision? I should be choosing outfits and changing nappies, complaining about lack of sleep, not any of this.

It just wasn't fair.

Midwives came and went, they removed my staples from my wound, asked questions about how my body was recovering, I went through the motions, but my mind wasn't there. I could've told them anything, it seemed stupid them being there without my baby to weigh and check on.

I saw my beautiful girl for the last time exactly a week after she was born, at the funeral directors, dressed in her beautiful butterfly dress, I placed a teddy and a photo of me and her dad in with her, told her how much I loved her and kissed her goodbye for the very last time.

Walking out of there was almost as difficult as walking out of the hospital without her, in fact, maybe more so. This isn't how life should be. There are no words to describe how it felt.

The day of her funeral – Thursday 2nd June – I remember it so clearly it could've been yesterday.

My sister had been and bought me some new clothes the day before as nothing fitted, and she did my hair for me, I had no energy to do anything for myself, I was still in a lot of pain from my caesarean and felt so uncomfortable.

There were lots of people at my mum's house that morning, I had left all my babies' photos and hand/footprints etc on the dining table for everyone to see, I was proud of my beautiful girl and wanted everyone to see her.

Only now do I realise that they probably didn't want to see those photos – only now, years down the line do I realise how uncomfortable people are when faced with baby loss. In fact, I would bet that most of those people really didn't want to be there.

I was surprisingly calm and composed, talking to people, showing them photos, putting on a smile.

I remember hearing somebody say, "the cars are here" and I made my way down the hallway to the front door...

Seeing the tiny white coffin and her name in flowers took my breath away, I could feel my legs giving way from underneath me and steadied myself on the nearest person to me.

Quite how I managed those few steps through the front garden and into the funeral car is beyond me.

It seemed like the whole street had come out to watch.

I felt like I was in some kind of freak show as I was helped into the car.

Arriving at the cemetery just a few minutes later I saw a huge crowd of people, there were a lot of people there to say goodbye to my beautiful girl, I remember feeling glad that so many people cared.

I'm unsure how I got through the funeral service, I remember being held up by my mum and my partner, crying silent tears.

I remember standing watching her tiny coffin being lowered into the ground, watching everybody else walk away and just wanting to stay there forever.

Eventually someone made me leave, and we went to the local pub for some food. I went through the motions, let people hug me and tell me how sorry they were, but my heart wasn't there, all I wanted to do was go home to bed and hide.

2 days after the funeral was my nannas 70th birthday party – I had insisted that it still go ahead but didn't think I'd be able to face going. But my nanna has always been a massive part of my life, so a little after everyone else had left I decided to make the effort, to get myself dressed and go along.

I remember walking into the party so clearly, it was as though the whole room went silent, nobody really said anything, everybody just looked at me – another part of me died in that moment, these people were all family and friends, but they didn't know what to say to me. It was although I had a contagious disease that no one wanted to catch.

I felt very lost.

I was so grateful to the couple of people who took it upon themselves to come and sit with me, to be normal and talk to me, and even more grateful to the person who during their speech acknowledged my beautiful girl.

Turns out that was just the start of things to come. This was normal for someone who has lost a baby, those feelings of being outcast, watching people cross over the road to avoid you, the friends that once were there just disappearing into nowhere.

Losing my beautiful baby girl was isolating.

The next few months are a bit of a blur, I somehow survived, I focused on making her grave look beautiful, creating somewhere special and nice to go and remember her.

Instead of buying tiny clothes and toys, I found myself choosing a headstone, and buying flowers, instead of rocking my baby to sleep at night I lay alone, in the dark crying myself to sleep.

At some point in those early weeks, I began to sort through the mountains of baby things we had bought whilst I was pregnant. I passed some of them on to my sister, but the majority were thrown away...I vividly remember spending one exceptionally long day listing lots of brand-new items on eBay – I sold all the beautiful winnie the pooh bedding I had spent weeks choosing – I could no longer bear to even look at it.

The agony of coming home from the hospital with no baby to a house full of baby equipment that will never be used is just another part of the torture of baby loss.

The cot all set up ready.

The wardrobe full of clothes.

The empty pram.

I still to this day have never bought any of my other children anything winnie the pooh – that's one thing that was only hers.

The only positive thing I did during those first few weeks was joining an online support group and through there I began to realise that what I was feeling was normal, that I wasn't alone. I spent all my days on there talking to other mums who had been through similar losses, we chatted for hours and hours every single day, they knew and understood how I was feeling, and we supported each other.

It was my lifeline.

By this point most people had stopped mentioning my baby, I had lost contact with the world, I saw nobody other than close family, and I spent my days at home, confined to the house.

9 weeks after she died, my sisters' baby was born, she had asked me if she had a girl if I minded her using my babies name as her middle name, and I felt honoured that she cared so much, that my baby girl would never be forgotten.

Although I cried sat alone in my room upon hearing she had had a little girl, and I had no idea how I would cope being around her, I threw myself straight into the deep end, went straight to the shops and bought some tiny pink clothes.

I felt sick knowing I should be doing this for my own baby, I can still see myself at the till with the lady behind the counter asking who they were for, but I went straight to the hospital to visit.

All my fears quickly went away though, as soon as I saw her, my initial feeling was of relief, relief that she was ok, she was alive and well, and very quickly after that came the relief that she didn't look like my baby.

I immediately fell in love with her.

I spent a lot of time with my newborn niece, looking after her somehow helped me to get through each day, she gave me something positive to focus on, a reason to get out of bed in the mornings, a reason to smile. She was one very spoilt little girl!

On the day of her christening, exactly 6 months since my baby had been born, my partner took his mum to the cemetery. Whilst at the christening I received a phone call telling me that the ornaments I had bought and placed on her grave had all been stolen – I was devastated.

I remember standing in the massive hall full of people and bursting into tears.

Not only had my baby been taken away for me, but someone had also taken it upon themselves to ruin her resting place. I was devastated.

The next day I did something I would never dreamed of doing before I became a mother – I went to the cemetery and had my photo taken by the local newspaper, they wrote an article about the ornaments being stolen – I put myself, and my grief out for the world to see, my motherly instincts took over and I wanted justice, I wanted whoever had done this to feel guilty, to realise how much hurt they had caused.

Gone was the shy person who wouldn't dream of letting the world see her, she had been replaced by a mother with a love so strong nothing else mattered.

I was a different person, stronger than I had been before, determined not to let anyone ruin the memory of my beautiful girl. I was still a mother, and although I had no baby to look after, I had to look after her memory.

FIVE

By this point I had met with the doctors who had looked after my baby girl and been told they had found no cause for her hydrops, all the tests had come back negative, that it was just "one of those things", that it wouldn't happen again. The odds were about 1 in a million they said...

So, we decided we wanted to have another baby – and almost immediately I was staring at a positive pregnancy test.

This pregnancy was hugely different to my first.

The feelings I had were hard to get my head round, I was scared, no longer naïve, and although I was excited for my new baby, I didn't want my new baby to replace the one I had lost, I wasn't sure I could love another baby like I had loved her.

I was well looked after though, I did attempt to go back to university during this pregnancy, but although I was being closely monitored, I was also no longer naïve, I was acutely aware of what could go wrong, and at 20 years old had already experienced the worst.

I just couldn't cope with university on top of everything else I had going on, and my outlook on life had changed. I knew now that there was no way on earth I would be sending my baby to nursery while I studied, I would be a full time mum, I knew that was the only way forward to me, university was no longer important, I was a mother, that was my job now, that was the only important thing in the world, looking after the new baby I was growing, and looking after the memory of my beautiful girl. That seemed like a full-time job, and one I knew I would continue with for the rest of my life.

This time I was only 26 weeks pregnant when a routine appointment once again showed I was measuring too big for my dates – this time I fought, I insisted on a scan that day (with some help from my mum) and lo and behold my instinct was right – against all odds, against everything the doctors had told me – this baby had hydrops too.

There was no offer of a termination this time, by now the consultant knew me well, and she knew my determination, she cared as much as we did that, we would have a healthy baby, and she did everything in her power to help that happen.

This time around there were 8 weeks of interventions, 8 whole weeks filled with hospital appointments, all of the same scans and tests that I had had last time round, but more of them. I was at the hospital every few days having more and more fluid drained from my stomach and babies' lungs.

This time around it was decided to try in-utero surgery to insert stents to drain fluid from the baby, miraculously it worked, and we could see the fluid draining on the ultrasound scan. Sadly, it was short-lived, as I managed to fall down the stairs and dislodge it only a few days later.

Those 8 weeks were filled with so many trips to hospital, countless painful amnio drainages, more tears than I could count, but also more love than could be measured.

Losing my beautiful girl had taught me how cruel life could be, how bad things can happen, but it had also taught me how to be a mother, how to fight for my babies, how to protect them.

SIX

On Wednesday 3rd May 2006, at 34 weeks and 5 days (the same gestation as his big sister) my biggest boy was born – again by planned caesarean section.

That morning I had been visited by the consultant neonatologist – who had sat on the end of my hospital bed and said "you do realise that this baby is probably going to die" his words cut straight to my heart, I was absolutely petrified.

I cried endless tears that day, I sat for hours receiving a blood transfusion as I was so anaemic, and my body was so weak they refused to take me to theatre until I had had a transfusion.

However, in that theatre, the very same one his sister had been born in exactly 49 weeks earlier, surrounded by what seemed like hundreds of strangers, my baby boy was born.

Expecting silence, I was stunned when I heard a tiny cry before he was whisked away – that tiny cry gave me hope, strength and even more determination to fight for him.

He was quickly taken into the neonatal intensive care unit, and once I was out of theatre and in recovery my consultant came to tell me that he had been ventilated and they were inserting chest drains.

My baby was alive!

My partner and my mum went to see him that night, once he had been made stable and they brought me back some polaroid pictures that the nurses had taken for me.

I still couldn't believe he had made it, that he was fighting.

It was nearly 24 hours before I could see him- I was too unwell, still recovering from the anaesthetic and still receiving a blood transfusion.

Once again, I was lay in my hospital bed, a new mother without her baby, though things were so very different now.

It took all my strength to get into the wheelchair to go and see him that next afternoon, but my love for him and my need to see him with my own eyes made me determined.

I was pushed through the hospital in a wheelchair, through those same corridors I had walked through without my baby less than a year ago.

We got out of the lift and into the NICU, parked the wheelchair outside the intensive care room and I used all my strength to stand up and hobble into the huge room.

I remember it being so bright, and incredibly busy, it was terrifying. I was taken to his incubator where I cried happy tears, he was so small - although he had weighed over 7 pounds at birth, a lot of that was fluid, he was on a ventilator, hooked up to so many machines.

He had chest drains, big, long tubes coming out from under each armpit draining into big containers on the floor. The doctor came to speak to me and told me he was incredibly poorly and fragile.... he couldn't breathe on his own. He had a long hard journey ahead of him.

But he was alive and fighting and that gave me more strength than I'd ever imagined possible.

The nurses in NICU were amazing. They took pictures of him and sent them up to the ward for me and kept me updated all the time. They told me that breastmilk would be good for him and showed me to a room where I could express some for him. I hadn't planned on breastfeeding but knowing it could help him made me do it. I hated every minute of pumping, but I did it for him.

Unfortunately, his battle wasn't an easy one. Although alive, my baby boy was extremely unwell, the hydrops had affected his lungs badly, he was kept in intensive care for the first 5 weeks of his life while he learnt to breathe on his own, there were many ups and downs.

The first time I got to hold him it was for a matter of seconds whilst his sheet was changed after a particularly messy nappy change (that is not easy in an incubator!) and I was terrified of all the wires and tubes.

The first time I got to breastfeed him he was nearly 2 weeks old, and I had absolutely no idea what I was doing, but the nurse put a screen round us and we muddled through.

That was short-lived, it was soon found that his condition meant his lymphatic system didn't work and he could not tolerate breastmilk, so after less than 3 weeks the pumping stopped and specialist formula was introduced – the change in him was almost immediate, the fluid stopped accumulating and he learnt to breathe on his own for longer periods.

He began to get stronger and was transferred out of intensive care and to our local hospital at 3 weeks old – on the day of his big sister's 1st birthday.

That was a bittersweet day, as we visited the cemetery, we watched for the ambulance passing us transporting our baby boy to our local hospital. I was thankful that it meant I could get to him more easily and spend much more time with him.

Whilst he was there, I learnt to tube feed him and use all his machines and tubes. He finally had his first bath at 4 weeks old and he was allowed to wear proper clothes, he was beginning to look like a real baby!

After 5 long weeks, he was almost ready to come home. First of all, both me, his dad and my family (who we lived with) were all taught infant resuscitation. Once we were confident with that, we got to take him for walks around the hospital grounds in a pram, getting used to his tubes and monitors, finally getting to show him the outside world. It was amazing.

A few days later, I got to sleep at the hospital with him for the night, the first night we had spent together, the first time I had been responsible for him, with the nurses there for back up to ensure I could use all of his equipment properly.

It was a long night where I didn't sleep at all, I was so happy to be there with him, but a little overwhelmed with everything I had to learn. But it was incredible, I finally felt like his mummy, just 2 days later he was finally allowed to come home!

His battle was far from over, not only had I become his mummy, but I also needed to be his carer.

The number of obstacles he overcame in his early years was huge.

At only a few weeks old at a routine appointment I was told he "probably couldn't see" – I spent weeks terrified that my baby had no sight, agonising over what his life would be like, only to be told a few weeks later they'd used the wrong test, he was far too young to have passed the first one as they hadn't taken his prematurity into account and in fact, his eyesight wasn't perfect, but he just needed glasses!

His immune system was extremely weak, and he picked up infection after infection, often requiring stays in hospital.

I had to learn how to use all his medical equipment, it soon became second nature, attaching tubes, changing oxygen cylinders, switching off alarming monitors, checking breathing rates and oxygen saturations was just everyday life.

I had to take him to a lot of medical appointments and soon realised I would have to advocate for him, to stand up for what he needed – I had to learn to speak up for not only myself, but for my baby too.

I could no longer shy away from social situations and strangers, I had to interact with medical professionals on an almost daily basis. I could no longer be hiding in the corner away from the world, I had to fight for my boy. And wow has he made me fight on some occasions!!!

At 18 months old a particularly bad chest infection caused his lung to collapse suddenly – luckily, my mother's instinct had told me there was something very wrong, and even after being discharged from the hospital with "a cold" that morning I took him back there just in time – I had to be his voice, I had to have confidence in myself to get what was right for my baby.

We very nearly lost him that night.

I still remember so clearly the look on the consultant's face as they rang a specialist hospital with intensive care facilities and began to arrange his transfer. I remember ringing my mum in tears from high dependency, where I lay all night in the hospital bed with him trying to keep him calm enough for his drips to stay in and work their magic.

My old self wouldn't have gone back to the hospital until it was too late, wouldn't have argued that they'd been wrong the first time they'd seen him that morning, wouldn't have made them listen. But the raging protective mother in me made sure I did.

I am so thankful that having my daughter changed me into a person strong enough to do that, strong enough to believe in myself and do the right thing.

I had become almost unrecognisable from my former self – I had gained a newfound confidence in getting what was needed for my children, a fighting spirit I never knew existed until my maternal instinct and the immense love for my children made it possible.

That hospital stay marked a massive step backwards in his health, a return to the full-time high flow oxygen we had managed to wean his off gradually over the past few months, but he quickly recovered and began to improve again in no time.

There have sadly been a few more occasions like this in the past 15 years, (though luckily not for several years as my biggest boy is now incredibly well – amazingly you would never guess the amount of stuff he went through when he was small and other than a couple of scars and asthma if you met him in the street (or more likely on the basketball court) you'd see an almost 6 foot tall young man without a care in the world!

There were so many occasions in the first 2-3 years of his life where I was looked down on by other people, where he was stared at whilst we were out, where people stopped what they were doing to watch him (and me), and I saw the pity in their eyes.

Yes, my boy looked different to others, yes, he had tubes on his face and a breathing monitor in his pram, yes, I was carrying round a heavy oxygen cylinder just to keep him alive, and yes sometimes I did park in the disabled parking space.... because it was IMPOSSIBLE to get a small baby, car seat and oxygen cylinder out of the car in a normal one sometimes!!

At first, all these differences made me want to hide him from the rest of the world, afraid of peoples stares and reactions, but slowly, and with the help of my family - especially my sister - I learnt to ignore the stares, to stare back, to not let it get to me.... I began to realise that some people were simply curious, not everybody was plain rude!

As he got bigger and started to walk this became more of an issue. It was incredibly difficult to let him walk whilst we were out of the house, running after him with his oxygen cylinder, him restrained by the tube across his face....I was too scared to let him do things other "normal" children his age were doing....to the point that one day my sister took him from me and took him to a soft play area herself, the first I knew was a photo she text me of him having a wonderful time!!

From this point I vowed to not let the stares and comments of other people hold him back, I made myself get over it and decided that me and my baby boy were going to get out more and enjoy life.

I'm not saying it was easy bringing up such a poorly child - it really wasn't, but in my head, this was amazing, I didn't care what I had to do, what obstacles were thrown at me, he was alive, and that was all that mattered. I was still overprotective of him though, in fact my friends and family still laugh about how neurotic I was, but I've come to realise that is just a part of who I am now, it's just a reaction to my past experiences, and I do try much harder nowadays to worry less....

My first 2 children changed me as a person, completely.

Gone was the person who just wanted to hide away from the world, the person who just wanted to live life quietly, to be in the background, to please everybody.

By the time he was 3 years old, and in a much better place health wise – he had finally been weaned off his home oxygen, I had realised that life is for living, for having fun, for cherishing each moment, for being happy.

I had changed, I was a completely different person to who I had been, I had some enormous life changing decisions to make.

It was at this point, when he was 3 years old, that I finally found the courage to start a new life, just me and my boy – I was no longer scared of being on my own and I wanted to enjoy life and be happy.

SEVEN

Not too long after starting our new life, I unexpectedly found myself pregnant and soon enough had another little man in my life.

Thankfully free from hydrops, with a relatively uneventful pregnancy and although he was born with a kidney condition, that required some traumatic tests in his first months of life, and 5 years' worth of antibiotics, compared to his brother and sister he was in incredibly good health.

This little man brought with him a whole different battle, and changed the person I am in a different, maybe an even bigger way.

Having him set me off on another journey, a completely different one, a journey of single parenting 2 small children, of moving into our own home and starting over.

There were moments where it was traumatic, but overall, it was amazing.

Parenting a healthy baby was a whole new thing for me, it was weird having no tubes or monitors, no endless hospital visits.... A completely different experience and I loved every moment.

I'm not going to go into detail with his story here, it's not something that he wants me to share, and of course that's up to him, but I will say that having him taught me that fighting for your children is sometimes necessary – literally.

Being his mummy brought out my fighting spirit, taught me that I can face even the toughest of challenges on my own, made me stand up for myself and for what is right, and most of all taught me that blood is not actually thicker than water.

Fighting for him gave me a newfound confidence, an ability to stand up and speak for myself, to talk to people I'd never have dreamed of talking to before, and eventually the confidence to put myself into situations I would have previously avoided at all costs.

I'm happy to say that after a long, hard battle, with many difficult decisions along the way, and with my new husband by my side, we found our happy ending.

He is 11 now and about to start high school, and is the most incredible boy, the kindest, most caring brother, and the biggest Daddy's boy I've ever known.

We must've done something right!

EIGHT

The next part of my journey started with a blog post. I had gone online looking for similar stories to what I found myself facing and read about so many women facing what I was who had told nobody, who had suffered alone, who were too ashamed to ask for help.

I nearly didn't write it, but then I thought back to the very first time I told my story... It took a lot of courage to publish, I was scared what people would think, what they would say, but I did it anyway.

I was passionate about allowing women to speak about their experiences, to seek comfort from one another, to share stories and to share their children, dead or alive.

I realised that since sharing my story I had received several messages from other women thanking me for telling my story, telling me how it's helped them in one way or another....

So, if me telling this next part of my story can help even just one person then to me it will have been worthwhile...

Initially I thought people may think I was just looking for sympathy, for attention. That is certainly not the case.... In fact, those that know me well will know I don't accept either sympathy or attention very well!!

But.

If I've learnt one thing since the beginning of my journey to motherhood, it's that silence doesn't help.

There are too many taboo subjects in our society and there really is no need... How else can other people seek comfort and advice when they're faced with a similar situation if they've no idea anyone else they know has been through similar.... How can it possibly help anyone to let people feel ashamed??!

I've been lucky in having a handful of supportive friends along my journey, some having experienced baby loss, and some my more recent events.... And I can honestly say their support has been invaluable.

So, here goes.

"This should've been a happy post.

You see, a few weeks ago me and hubby got the most amazing news.... Just 4 weeks after being told it was unlikely, we would ever conceive without IVF, after a long 3-year battle with "unexplained fertility" and numerous rather unpleasant tests and procedures and trying to face my fear of taking tablets to force down fertility drugs that may or may not help, we found out I was pregnant!

Considering it's something we'd both wanted for such a long time it came as a shock to us both!

We'd just about got our heads round the fact it was never going to happen. But we were so incredibly happy.

Nervous too of course, especially knowing there was a 50% chance of me passing on the same gene that my 2 eldest children have.... But excited, positive, happy, hopeful....

The journey to get this far had been tough, there had been many tears shed and so much heartache.

Fast forward a few weeks.... We'd told close family and a couple of close friends the good news, I was feeling awful, all day sickness, exhausted, but happy....

At 8 weeks pregnant I booked in with the midwife... That was eventful.

My pregnancy history is possibly one of the most complicated. All 3 of them had some kind of problem, most of which didn't fit into any of the obligatory tick boxes. It was the poor midwifes first ever booking appointment, I really hope I didn't put her off. (She did have a mentor with her for guidance and luckily had a good sense of humour but I'm guessing that after 2 whole hours she probably needed a strong drink!)

2 days later I was booked in for a "reassurance scan" due to having taken fertility drugs.... The appointment was at 7am and I was exhausted, feeling sick and ridiculously nervous.... Hubby was extremely excited as we stood in the dark room and waited for our lovely fertility nurse to scan me.

All was quiet for a few seconds until she said, "is there any chance you could be less far along than you think?" In that second my heart sank.... I knew from that very second it was not good news.... There was absolutely no way my dates could be wrong.... 3 years of tracking and 4 months of drug taking made me 100% positive....

After a couple more silent minutes of me gripping hubby's hand so incredibly tightly she finally told us.... Although she could see a baby, she couldn't see a heartbeat, although there was a flickering on the screen, she didn't think it was fast enough and was probably my own heartbeat rather than the baby's....

She explained that it wasn't necessarily bad news, but that she would have to rescan me in 2 weeks to see if there had been any progress …. Luckily, she later changed her mind and booked the appointment for 1 week later to save my sanity.

I cried many tears that day, I knew that it was bad news immediately, hubby didn't believe it, he was hopeful, as was my mum, but I just knew.

The next week was possibly the longest of my life, I didn't leave the house, stayed in my pjs petrified that the inevitable was going to happen at any point, too afraid for it to happen when I wasn't at home.

Luckily, we had great family around us, my mum, sister and mother-in-law all stepped in, looking after the boys, taking them to school and picking them up, taking them out over the weekend to give us a break.

Eventually the following week arrived.

Me and hubby arrived at the hospital, this time not so early, and it was crazily busy. The 45 minutes we sat waiting for the scan seemed like days.

The silence from the sonographer, combined with the fact she switched off the screen before speaking to us confirmed what I already knew…. Our baby had died.

I was surprisingly calm, there were no tears, I think I had already processed what had happened during the week of waiting. Hubby on the other hand looked broken. He had been hopeful, he hadn't believed them last week, he was waiting for them to tell us everything was fine. I felt sad for him more than myself, I just wanted to make things better.

We were sent back to the busy waiting room for another half an hour while we waited to see a nurse. Eventually she took us into a room and explained our options.... It was decided they would book me in for an ERPC ASAP.

We went home and waited for the phone call, desperately hoping they could do it the next day rather than wait over the weekend again. Thankfully, our wishes were answered, and they rang and booked me in.

We made the decision to tell the boys what had happened that night, after a lot of thinking, we decided the truth was the only option.

At first, I was worried, worried how they'd take it, worried that they'd be upset, then worried that they would tell everyone, and I'd be the talk of the playground.

I soon concluded that that didn't matter. What mattered was my boys, and them understanding and being ok. Biggest boy had been clearly struggling all week anyway, he obviously knew there was something wrong and was worried about me.

The look of relief when we told him was amazing.... In that split second, I knew we had made the right choice, he later told me "I thought you had cancer or something" my poor boy had clearly been affected much more than we realised.

That taught me an important lesson. Our children deserved to be told the truth – age appropriately of course – but they took in more than we gave them credit for. They too could learn from our life experiences, hiding them from hurt and sadness was definitely not a good idea.

So what if they told people? I'm not ashamed. Sadly, this happens to a lot of people, it's something that doesn't need to be hidden away from the world".

NINE

We arrived at the hospital at 7am on a Friday morning. I was admitted as a day case, the staff were amazing and found me a side room so that hubby could stay with me, something I will be eternally grateful for.

I was booked in and told I was 3rd on the list.

The doctor came to see us and explained what would happen, we had to make a decision about what to do with the "remains". I must admit that part caught me completely off guard, I hadn't even contemplated what would happen.

We agreed that the remains would be cremated and put in our local cemetery's baby garden.

I was given some tablets at 11am – no one really said what for other than to prepare me for surgery – but I'd soon find out.

Minutes turned into hours and there was still no sign of me going anywhere, the anaesthetist hadn't been to see me yet, I was told there had been an emergency and they didn't know how long it would be.

By 3pm I was still sat in my boiling hot, windowless room. I was nil by mouth and by now starting to feel quite dehydrated and rubbish. The lovely ward manager came to see us and apologised, she said she was trying to fit me onto a different consultants list because the emergency before me was still in theatre and would be there for a while.

Half an hour passed, and she came back to say that she was sorry, they couldn't fit me on the other list either, they'd had to put me on the evening list instead.... I cried. I just wanted to get it over with and get home and cuddle my boys.

By 4pm the drama started.

The inevitable began to happen.

The lovely nurse came and explained that the tablets I'd been given that morning were for the "medical management of miscarriage" that I'd waited too long to go to theatre so instead of just softening the cervix ready for the operation they'd started to work.

By 4.30pm I was in agony, I'll spare the details but after the nurse made a phone call I was put into a wheelchair and taken straight to theatre as an emergency.

The staff who greeted me were lovely, they got me straight onto a trolley and hooked me up to pain relief and fluids, they were surprised at how dehydrated I was and did their best to cheer me up as I waited to go into the anaesthetic room.

Only then did they realise the anaesthetist hadn't seen me on the ward in the morning as they were meant to, which meant we had to wait even longer to get the paperwork sorted.

Thankfully, the next thing I remember is waking up at 5.45pm and being taken back to the ward, relieved it was finally all over and desperate to get home.

I was finally allowed out of bed at 8pm although even that was quite eventful and led to hubby escaping very quickly from the cubicle! I was looked after so well by amazing staff though, and finally got home to my own bed.

I had naively thought that after having surgery I would recover quickly and be back to normal after the weekend.... I couldn't have been more wrong!

Emotionally I was doing ok, but physically was a completely different story, hubby was still off work days later as I literally could not function.

Hours of unbearable contractions each day, barely touched by pain killers, leaving me literally sobbing in pain and exhaustion.... I could barely walk up and down the stairs never mind do the school run.

I was cheered up by friends and family dropping off cards and gifts, it was nice to know people cared and were thinking of us.

I finally got a negative pregnancy test 2 weeks after my surgery, my body had finally started to get back to normal, though in that moment I couldn't decide if I should be happy or sad?!

Happy that I was recovering, that I was getting back to normal, sad that I should still be pregnant.... But I couldn't dwell on that for long.

TEN

Just a couple of short weeks later, and physically and emotionally I had healed well.

If you had asked me then if my journey would continue, honestly, the answer would have been I don't know.

What I did know is that I was determined to come out of all this stronger, if there was one thing my journey so far had taught me it was not to give up, but more importantly, it had taught me to be thankful for what I had, to cherish every moment with my children. And that's exactly what I planned on doing.

It was the end of the school year and I was making plans for lots of fun with my boys, when out of nowhere the sadness hit me. It didn't happen that often these days, it had been 11 years since my baby died, it was something I lived with relatively easily these days, but suddenly, reading all my friends posts about their children leaving primary school, about all the plays, trips, discos, services.

It hit me hard.

All those things I would have... could have... SHOULD have been doing with my beautiful girl.... She too would be at the end of year 6, getting ready to move on to high school, who knows what she'd have been like?

I could only imagine.

The sadness was few and far between by then, but there was still the odd occasion, moment, or event that knocked me sideways, like this whole leaving primary school thing, but I was glad in a way, it showed my love for her hadn't faded over time, her memory was very much still alive.

Several people had told me how strong I was since my most recent loss, but I didn't feel strong.

I was just a mother, doing all I could for my children and my family. Giving up simply wasn't an option.

Summer was my favourite time of year, I was one of these weird mums who loved having the kids off school, enjoyed spending my days on the park, loved making memories for my boys.

This was probably because I was well aware that memories are so important, that one day memories would be all we had.

Although being a full-time parent was tough, in fact some days it was pretty impossible and I couldve quite happily banged their heads together, scream shout and run away, the moments of happiness were worth it all (I kept telling myself this!!)

I wanted them to enjoy every day, to smile and be as carefree as possible, and usually the summer was the easiest time for that, endless days spent doing whatever we fancied, picnics in the park or jumping in the puddles.

I was the most irritating mum, with the camera always out, always taking photos so that we could look back at them – they hated it, but I wasn't sorry.

No one ever regretted taking photos – I definitely regret not taking enough though.

This summer hadn't quite been like that.

Over the course of the summer months, I had had a miscarriage, hubby had had an operation which required 3 1/2 weeks off his feet and off work without pay, my nan passed away, and we had moved to a new house.

Parenting is hard.

Parenting whilst grieving is harder.

Parenting a grieving child whilst grieving is really fucking shit.

I made the decision to tell the boys that nan didn't have very long left, that they probably only had that day to see her before she might not be there anymore.

Smallest boy didn't want to go and see her – completely his choice, but biggest boy chose to visit my nan in her final hours, not once but twice.

He came to see her the first time, he was obviously scared, but he sat with her and held her hand, told her he loved her and kissed her goodbye.

I sobbed as I saw how grown up he had become, as I realised, he wasn't quite as innocent as I had thought, as I saw in his eyes that he knew her end was near, and he needed to say his goodbyes.

He left with his dad while I stayed, but then later rang and asked to come back, he returned just an hour before she died, and gave her one final kiss.

My little boy suddenly seemed so grown up as he stood comforting my mum.

It was then, in that moment, I knew I'd done something right.

That inside that 10-year-old, attitude filled whirlwind was a lovely kind and caring young man who understood and felt far more than we gave him credit for.

He cried himself to sleep for several nights after nan died, and sleepwalked for the first time in his life, he was grieving hard, but all along he kept telling me he was so glad he had got to say goodbye.

He made me realise I'd done the right thing in telling him the truth, telling him that nans end was close. Being honest with him allowed him to make a decision and choose to visit and say goodbye.

I'm so glad I allowed him that opportunity.

I knew my beautiful nan would be so proud of us all, and though we had grieved for her quite some time ago when we lost her to Alzheimer's, we were grieving all over again, she was "simply the best" and we would all miss her terribly, but she taught us how important family is, she went through some very tough times herself and she came out smiling.

There was a lot to be learnt from such an amazing woman.

So, that summer had been tough, hard work and completely exhausting.

There aren't enough swear words to explain just how shit it had been in fact.

But as September began, we had moved into our new home and it was all coming together nicely (after a lot of hard work) the boys were back at school and settling into their new classes well and hubby had just got back to work too.

So, I began to look forward to Autumn and hope that it brought some relief from all the drama we had endured recently....

I was hoping for a quiet life, for a little while at least!

ELEVEN

A few months later, I went to the premiere of a documentary about baby loss, I had been in contact with the director briefly to help with her previous short film about baby loss, sent her photos of my memory box and scrapbook to give her ideas for props, and had travelled to Sheffield for the premiere of the short film.

I had been following her work ever since and was thrilled that there was a local screening. One of my dear friends and her family were featuring in this documentary and I couldn't wait to watch.

I must admit I was nervous, and not sure what to expect. But what I saw was real, it was real people sharing their very real experiences, their innermost thoughts, their most precious memories, photos and videos, baring their deepest darkest thoughts for the world to see.

There was no glossing over bits, it was frank and open, and bloody difficult.

It was definitely not an easy watch, and probably not quite what I was expecting, it showed the harsh realities of losing a baby, and the emotions, heartache and changes that happen in the days/months and even years afterwards.

It aimed to raise awareness of what so many people go through, of all the things that just aren't talked about, and although at times dark, and deeply upsetting it does show the reality for those of us who have lived through that journey.

It showed parts that even I haven't shared with my closest friends, the families involved have every bit of my respect for allowing the world into the depths of their hearts and lives, to see those bits that even I can't let people in to.

Sadly, I didn't expect anyone who hasn't experienced baby loss would go and watch... the question-and-answer session with the director and professionals at the end of the screening echoed that.... the main tv channels won't show it as basically "nobody wants to see photos of a dead baby", and I guess they're right.... unless you've been through baby loss then why would you?

12 years earlier there is no way I would have watched something so stark, honest and heart wrenching.

The thought of seeing photos/videos of a dead baby would have sent me running for miles, the image of a tiny coffin and a wailing mother would've made me switch off.... and I imagine most of my friends would feel the same now – I don't blame them, and I completely get that... for all those who haven't walked this journey the footage shown in the documentary is hellish.... but it is reality for the families shown in the film, MY reality, and the reality of so many more people than you would imagine.

This film showed the horrendous journey in the most honest way possible, but there's not many people who want to see that...the majority of people don't want to even imagine that it happens, don't want to even try and understand the journey of baby loss.... and I completely get that.

There were many professionals at the screening though, all of whom seemed united in wanting to change the experience of baby loss and help grieving parents, to treat those parents and their babies with the dignity, respect and compassion they deserve.

I count myself as one of the "lucky" ones…. obviously not lucky in the loss of my beautiful girl, but lucky in the time I spent with her and the care I received in the hospital, I know of many others whose experiences were far worse.

In a weird turn of events, the last person to ask a question was sat just behind me, she introduced herself, and I turned round to watch her. I immediately recognised her as the midwife who was with me when my baby girl was born, who looked after us both and helped create the memories that I will hold forever.

I got to speak to her afterwards, which was bizarre after 11 years. Looking back, I didn't say any of the things I should have said.

She was now a specialist midwife dealing with baby loss and subsequent pregnancies in a new "rainbow clinic" and truly passionate about the treatment of parents and their babies.

I was one of the lucky ones who was cared for by someone like her, 11 years earlier not many of these midwifes seemed to exist.

Hopefully, this film would help in raising awareness- even if the audience is only small, if even that small number of people take on board the experiences of those in the film, it will help more people who must endure this horrendous journey to be cared for in the best way possible.

It would help more people to speak out, to talk about their experiences, to share their precious children and their memories with the world. If it made a difference to even one person going through baby loss, then it had been successful in my eyes.

I was so incredibly proud of my lovely friend and her family for taking part in this, and I desperately hoped that it would make a difference.

It would never bring back our babies, but their memories, and sharing our experiences could help so many others.

TWELVE

After our miscarriage in July, we had decided to wait a few months before making any kind of decision, we'd decided that after Christmas we would decide whether to start back on the fertility drugs and trying again.

Then, on Thursday 6th October I got up feeling something wasn't quite right, something made me take a pregnancy test, even though my head was telling me it wasn't possible, after all we were infertile, we couldn't get pregnant without help…. that blue line soon shut my head up…. I was pregnant.

I don't think hubby believed me at first when I rang him, I think he was more shocked than I was…. but it had really happened.

Immediately though, fear kicked in, I was terrified.

It took me over a week to make a Drs appointment, and then I couldn't bring myself to make a midwife appointment.

My GP offered me an early scan, but after last time we decided we couldn't go back to the hospital early in the morning because the boys would know straight away where we'd gone, so hubby booked a private early scan for Halloween instead.

All day sickness began, and exhaustion like I've never known before, I literally could not keep my eyes open past 7pm, and the smallest of tasks left me absolutely shattered…. the only time I stopped feeling sick was when I was eating, and I developed a love for salt and vinegar crisps!

I lived pretty much in denial up until the day of the scan, unable to really talk about it at all, and completely convinced that we would get there and find a baby with no heartbeat once again.

The morning of the scan came, and I could barely function, I was so scared I couldn't make myself get ready to go, but with a stern talking to from hubby we finally made it there.

Luckily, we didn't have to wait around, as soon as we arrived, we were taken straight in, and the sonographer sensed how nervous I was and lay me straight down for scan.... within seconds we could see a tiny little heart beating away.... a tiny baby, 8 weeks and 1 day along.... perfect.... we both cried happy tears.

I went to my first midwife appointment, which was uneventful until she took blood, and I wouldn't stop bleeding, 20 minutes later and a lot of pressure and cotton wool and it finally gave up! I received a consultant appointment for a few weeks' time.

Fast forward only a couple of weeks to that magical 12-week mark... everything is fine once you get to that point right!?

Wrong.

A Saturday night trip to A&E with bleeding, then an emergency Sunday morning scan and the news that our baby had no heartbeat.

All was fine on the 8-week scan.

How?

How could this be happening again?

I couldn't quite believe we had got to 12 weeks this time, that magic 12 weeks where everything was meant to be ok, that even after an amazing scan at 8 weeks, and getting to see the heartbeat, that we got all the way to 12 weeks before the world came crashing down.

Telling biggest boy what had happened was tough, he tried his best to be brave but later broke down and sobbed "I was looking forward to having a baby brother or sister".

The guilt for putting him through this again was immense. I think that was the worst part if I'm honest, as sad as I was, and as much as I was hurting, seeing the effect it had on other people was really fucking hard.

Another stand out moment which made me REALLY cross... whilst waiting for an emergency scan, I had to give my history to a nurse. Upon explaining about my previous missed miscarriage, I went on to tell her about my children, I explained that I had had 3 children but that my daughter had died shortly after birth.... something I had had to do many times before.

"Oh, an almost stillbirth then" was her response, and I watched completely dumb struck as she wrote that in my notes.

In the 11 years since having my baby girl I had heard some pretty thoughtless, stupid comments, many of which had come from medical staff.... but I'd never had the pleasure of that one before!

An "almost stillbirth" .... It doesn't even make sense!

Surely a baby is either born alive or it isn't?!

You'd think somebody working in maternity, in an emergency pregnancy loss clinic would be a bit more knowledgeable, have a little more compassion.... had I been in a better frame of mind I would have corrected her but sat awaiting confirmation that my baby had died I just didn't have the energy.

Hubby was incredibly cross about it when we got out of the room though, he was as stunned as I was at what she had said.

Luckily after the scan, the nurse was lovely, clearly just clueless about baby loss, as are so many.... which just made me more determined to keep on trying to do my bit to raise awareness.

Now I had to use every ounce of strength I could find to get through the next few days, to hope my body did what it should so I could avoid surgery, and to keep things as normal as I could for my boys. I knew it would be tough, but I had to be strong for them.

THIRTEEN

Thursday 1st December. That date that had been on our minds for the past few weeks. 12 weeks and 4 days pregnant, scan at 10.20am.

In a cruel twist of fate, we were indeed sat in maternity that morning at 10.20am, having just had a scan.... a scan to make sure the miscarriage that started on Saturday was complete.

In my body's true style, the news of course was not good.... and despite the events of the past few days the baby was still firmly intact.

Anger was my main emotion that day, from the nurse who had no idea why we were at the early pregnancy unit, making us relive every detail since Saturday... to the heavily pregnant women stood smoking in the doorway to maternity.

I was just angry at the whole world.

3 1/2 years down the line.... 3 years to get pregnant and now twice within 5 months we had lost our babies.... getting to 12 weeks this time just seemed so cruel.

I am happy to report that this time around the surgery and hospital stay were much better.

The staff were amazing once more, they made sure I was in a private room, that hubby was with me right up until I went to theatre and made sure I was first on the list, so I didn't have to sit in pain for too long.

Even when I ended up spending an extra almost 2 hours in recovery surrounded by Drs and nurses, they went straight to tell hubby, so he didn't worry too much, and they kept me calm even though there was obviously something wrong.

I ate my first ever hospital food – (it was only toast, and I was starving!) and they wheeled me out to go home and recover in peace as soon as they could.

It made such a difference being so well cared for and not having to deal with some of the stupid comments I had endured over the past week.

Recovery seemed to be quicker this time too, after only a few days I managed to do the school run - just!

I had to take a step back and realise what was important though.

What's important is that I got out of the house, my boys had normality, the excitement on littlest boy's face when he saw I'd come to pick him up was worth every ounce of the pain it resulted in.

The reality was that life goes on....

It may be tough to deal with sometimes, but it does.

There were still jobs to be done, tea to be made, washing to be done, and just because the world had stopped for me for a while didn't mean it had for anyone else.

I was glad in a way – I wouldn't wish this kind of pain (physical or emotional) on anyone, and although a tiny selfish part of me wished the world could just stop and let me get off for a while, wished I wasn't sat alone all day everyday with only my thoughts and a hot water bottle for company.... wished I could just switch off the world and avoid everyone else's happy posts and wonderful lives.

BUT I couldn't and I wouldn't do any of those things because that's just not me…. I couldn't be selfish, and I couldn't let anyone else suffer because of my pain…. I carried on for my boys, I took them to school and picked them up again even though that meant I spent the rest of the day curled up exhausted and in pain, because they were more than worth it.

I sat with them while they wrote their Christmas cards, and I gave in to their pestering to put up the tree (eventually!!) even though I couldn't muster even the slightest enthusiasm for Christmas, because they deserved it.

I watched from a distance whilst the rest of the world kept on going, tried my best to smile at the happy posts and have sympathy with the not so happy ones… because I knew that soon enough, I'd have bounced back, and the world would have gone on turning.

My experiences would serve a purpose one day I was sure, I would learn from them, I already had, and maybe one day somewhere along the line someone else would benefit from what I had learnt…. if I could make a difference to one person that had to go through this in the future then I guess that made it a little easier to bear – at least I hoped one day it would feel that way.

If my journey to motherhood had taught me anything it was that I could survive anything, yes, it was tough and in that moment, I wasn't scared to admit that I was struggling to find that elusive light at the end of the tunnel …. in fact, I was pretty sure there had been a power cut.

But I knew it was there, and it wouldn't be long until I found it again.

FOURTEEN

2016 saw the loss of my beautiful nan, being told we would probably never conceive without ivf, shortly followed by getting pregnant, and suffering missed miscarriages twice.... to say it was tough is a bit of an understatement.

2017 should have been the year we finally had the baby we had been longing for for almost 4 years... 28th January being our first due date and 12th June the second.

It wasn't all bad though, 2016 saw us move into our new house, and although making it our home was tough, it was worth it.

Waking up on the first day of a new year after nowhere near enough sleep, when both boys climbed into bed with us, I was reminded of all that we had.

Yes, in the past year we had lost a lot, there had been a lot of sadness, but we had also gained a lot too.

We must remember what we still had, we had each other, our beautiful, loving, irritating, exhausting little family.... Our lovely new home, and lots of fun to be had.

Onwards and upwards!

The new year new start positivity lasted approximately 2 hours... at which point I received a text from my GP surgery reminding me of my midwife appointment a few days later – I had asked them to cancel it weeks earlier, it's probably lucky it was New Year's Day, and they were closed because I'm not sure I could've hidden my anger with them had I been able to ring in that moment.

I guess I should have had some compassion, laugh it off, mistakes happen of course, and it could've been much worse, I just wished it didn't always seem to be us on the receiving end of other people's stupidity.

I did eventually calm down and realised it could've happened to someone not as strong as I am, and ruined more than just their afternoon, though I was still seriously annoyed!

So, the first day of the new year was harder work than it should've been, but luckily it was spent snuggled with my 3 favourite people, eating far too much and doing far too little... desperately clinging to the tiny shred of hope I had left that this wasn't the start of things to come, the beginnings of another shite year.

FIFTEEN

Parenting is a tough job, whatever the family circumstances it's not easy.

We're not the "typical" family, we didn't get married and then have our children together and live happily ever after, that's just not how our lives worked out.

I have no regrets, I am certainly not ashamed, that's just how it is for our family and it works.

We are a family, we work together, we parent together.

Yes, it's hard work at times, in fact it's bloody tough a lot of times, but I don't think I know any other parent in any other situation who would say anything different.... we all love each other, we respect each other, we laugh together and cry together, and we are all happy.... that's what's important right?

Biology is not important in this house... and all our children – I emphasise OUR children, regardless of biology, regardless of anything, are all treated equally,

There are so many different types of family now, and I can honestly say I don't think there's much difference between any of them. As long as the children within each family are loved, safe and treated fairly, I see no reason for any situation to work any better than another.

I have experienced been a single parent.

We have both experienced being separated parents, sharing our children with their other parent.

We have both become "stepparents" to each other's eldest children.

Between us, and those around us we have experienced or know of others experiences of many different family situations, and ways of parenting.

From adoptive parents, foster parents, single mothers, and single fathers, married parents, unmarried parents, happy parents, unhappy parents, young parents, old parents, same sex parents, shared care arrangements, other family members acting as parents.

Planned families and unplanned families, poor parents and rich parents, working parents, stay at home parents and many other kinds of parents.

Every single one of those parents finds it tough. Every single family is unique and has their own struggles. No one is qualified to judge. Regardless of circumstances, as parents we all still have the very same day to day struggles, no one is immune to it and as long as our children are loved who am I, or anyone else to judge??

I have nothing against those "perfect families" of people who have gone down the "traditional route" of getting married, buying a house and having children.... in fact, several of my closest friends have this kind of family and it works for them and they are happy. Of course, that is fantastic for them and for their children (not to mention far less complicated for all those involved!) BUT I am not envious of them, that's not how my life was meant to be and I'm perfectly happy with how mine turned out.

No matter how you choose to parent, no matter what the situation, no matter what relationships there are, what choices are made – it is both amazing and hard in equal measure.

I honestly wouldn't change our family for anything, complicated and untraditional as it may be, in fact it's been suggested by (incredibly rude) people in the past that it's more complicated than a soap opera!

Complicated it may be.... but there's a hell of a lot of love enclosed in it, and at the end of it all it is OUR family, they are OUR children, and we couldn't be any happier.

I should point out that we are incredibly lucky that all our children have loving grandparents and great grandparents, who regardless of genetics and blood love each of our children and treat them all equally.

Sadly, this isn't always the case, and for some reason some people just "don't get" stepfamilies and adoption. We personally have endured some ridiculous comments, and sadly we are not alone in that, I know of many stories of family members just not accepting children into their families because of a lack of genetic link.

Once upon a time maybe I was just as naive and misinformed as some others seem to be (though id like to think not, and I'm not sure I'd have been stupid enough to actually say things out loud!) However, I will go into a little of my own personal experience as maybe that has skewed my expectations somewhat.

My own parents split up when I was 16, it's no secret to those that know my family that life in our family home hadn't been particularly happy for some time before that, and I think I can speak for all of us when I say that life became easier after that point.

A year or so later my mum met someone new, and before long we were introduced to him. I'd like to think me, and my sister were nice to him from the beginning (though I may be corrected on this!), he moved in after a while and became a part of our family.

I can honestly say that when I became pregnant with my daughter a few months later there was NEVER any doubt that this man was to be my child's grandad, not on his part nor on mine. He was my mums' partner, they lived together, he was a big part of our lives, regardless of blood these children were going to be his grandchildren. And that is just how it has always been. No hesitation, no questions asked, it's just taken as given.

When my daughter was born and died, he was one of the very few people who was there for me, he came to the hospital, he held my beautiful girl and he cried.

I know he won't be ashamed for me to say that, because blood and genetics played no part in those feelings, only love. He had lost his precious granddaughter; genetics played no part in his love.

When my sons were born, he was once again one of the first visitors, and he has since become a VERY important person in their lives. He is an AMAZING grandad, and my boys adore him, as he does them. He often looks after them and they all love it. In their eyes he is their grandad, they know he isn't my dad, they know he isn't related to them genetically but THEY DONT CARE.... because that's not important to them, love is what's important, and they couldn't wish for any more of that from him.

Over the years this man became a father figure to me, he didn't replace my biological dad (that's not what stepparents are about), but he has given me more love and support than I could ever hope for. He had been there through every single high and low of life (and as I'm sure you've realised by now – there had been a few!)

Perhaps I'm just luckier than most?

Perhaps my own experiences of having a stepparent have clouded my judgement?

Although I must point out here that I was an adult before my stepdad became a part of my life. He didn't have to play a part in my life, I wasn't a small child requiring love and attention, I already had a dad of my own (regardless of our relationship), but he CHOSE to love me like his own, he CHOSE to be a grandparent to my children (and to my stepdaughter too).

I guess this positive experience raised my expectations of the general population and their reactions to stepfamilies and adoptive families.

I guess I thought as that's what my experience had been like then that's how everyone would react?

I guess I just like to expect the best in people.

Being loved and supported by my stepdad meant SO much to me (and still does of course) and as I have got older and have experienced the different relationships within our own little family it has made me appreciate him even more. Whenever we need him he is here to help, no questions asked. He doesn't have to do that, he doesn't have to even acknowledge us as his family, but he does, because we are.

This is exactly the kind of relationship I crave for our children, and of course within the walls of our house that is exactly how it is.

Blood and biology mean nothing…. stepCHILD, adopted CHILD, biological CHILD…. CHILD is the important bit the rest is irrelevant.

I'm happy to say that the majority of people in our lives have that same opinion, and our children love and respect them for that.

Biggest boy once, several years ago told us "I am so happy I was treated just like the others even though I'm not". His comment made us step back and really think.

It also made us even more passionate about the equality in our house, as soon enough the younger children would be just as mature and just as observant, and we vowed to do whatever we could to make sure that none of them would ever have a reason to make that kind of comment again. To make them feel that they would never be treated any differently to one another, for them to know that they are all equal, equally special, equally treated, and equally loved.

(Biased I may be!!) but all our children are amazing, each in their own individual ways, and to be a part of their lives is fantastic. From sharing in their good days and celebrations, to doing the mundane day to day stuff, and dealing with their tantrums and tears, even though a lot of the time it doesn't feel like in that moment, it is all incredibly rewarding, and the love shared is immense.

Our family may be formed differently to most, but for our children I don't think that is a disadvantage, they have all gained a bigger family, and more love and support than most children could ever imagine. Our children growing up with such close relationships, not only with us and each other, but with their cousins, their family and their friends has got to be the biggest positive of our unconventional family.

We know that they will always have someone to turn to, somewhere to go, somewhere to run away to when they're in trouble (yes that has already happened with biggest boy!!) because they are surrounded by love.

There's no such thing as too much love or support, right?!

Blood... water... water.... blood.... who really cares?

SIXTEEN

The due dates of my miscarriages were strange days.

It was weird to think had things been different we would have had a newborn.

Of course, I was sad, but weirdly not as sad as I thought I would be?

But I survived.

I was still smiling.... I had my amazing family to thank for that.

Mother's Day was a whole different level.

Social media was full of people's grand plans for Mother's Day, of the extravagant gifts they wished to receive, of the meals, the days out, the lie ins.... the expectations of some people were immense!

I could remember my first Mother's Day clearly.

March 2006. 10 months after I became a mother for the first time.

I spent most of the day in bed and in tears, you see I was a mother without a child.

I wasn't the proud owner of a handmade card and present, I was grieving, and I didn't feel like a mother at all.

I guess I was "lucky" at this time that social media wasn't a part of my life, that I didn't have to witness everybody else's perfect day, as I'm sure those people starting their baby loss journey right now are exposed to so much more than I was back then.

Mother's Day wasn't exactly my favourite day of the year, in many ways it was just a harsh reminder of what should have been and of what I had lost, although I'm happy to admit that it was much easier to bear these days than it was all those years ago, but still, whether 1 year or 100 years have passed those feelings of grief and loss don't just disappear.

Having my boys certainly made it easier and gives a timely reminder of all the things I do have, and how lucky I am to be their mummy, but I will ALWAYS spend Mother's Day without one of my children, that's never going to be easy.

Sadly, it doesn't stop there... it's not just people who have suffered the loss of a child that find Mother's Day hard, of course those people who have lost their own mother may also struggle, whether it's the 1st year or the 51st year without them, its still going to be tough.

Those battling infertility may struggle too, I know my situation was different, as in the 3 years we spent battling it we already had children, but it was still tough, so I can only imagine how difficult it must be for the thousands of people desperately wanting a child of their own.

Mother's Day is also tinged with the sadness of what could have been, with the loss of the 2 babies I miscarried. I'm sure it will be hard for very many other people who have suffered early pregnancy losses.

I guess what I'm trying to say is, spare a thought for other people, ITS NOT A COMPETITION!! It's not all about the best present or the longest lie in…. it's about love, about spending time together, about making and cherishing memories…. it's about appreciating how lucky we are to have our children, and our mothers, how lucky we are to be mothers.

I may have been through hell and back, I may have suffered the loss of my beautiful girl, I may have battled infertility, and I may have suffered miscarriages…

BUT I understand not everybody is as lucky as I am.

I still have my own mum.

I get to spend Mother's Day with my living children.

And for both of those things I am eternally grateful.

SEVENTEEN

A few short months later, we found ourselves leaving home at 6.40am for a trip to the hospital.

4 times we had sat in the early pregnancy unit within the past year, and 4 times I had left in tears.

That little room had been the scene for much bad news.

I have to say that by the time we went into the ultrasound room at 7.15am I had pretty much given up all hope, after all our odds so far had been 4/4, they don't get much better than that!

However, by some kind of miracle, within seconds of lying on the bed the lovely nurse said, "I can see a heartbeat, you can relax now".

A perfect little baby, conceived without the help of fertility treatment, in fact, conceived when we had stopped trying and resigned ourselves to the fact that our family was complete, with a perfectly beating heart, 8 weeks along and due on Christmas Day.

We had got to this point before of course, but we had a tiny glimmer of hope to hold onto now, we had 3 long weeks until our next scan, on my nan's birthday in fact, so we just had to keep our fingers crossed and hope that this was it, that this was our third time lucky, our happy ever after, surely even we deserved a happy ending by now?

It had been 4 years almost to the day since me and hubby made the enormous decision to try for another baby, a decision which had taken probably another year before that to make. Pregnancy was never going to be an easy ride for us, after all by that point I'd already had 3 Caesareans and had lost my darling girl. We knew at that point that there's a 50% chance of any future babies being affected by the same condition as both of my eldest children, so it wasn't a decision we took lightly.

After much discussion and soul searching, a year of indecision, we decided to go for it, we decided we were strong enough to deal with whatever was thrown at us, but we had absolutely no idea what would happen over the next 4 years, we were fully prepared for a high-risk pregnancy, with lots of consultant involvement and lots of stress and worry from 20 weeks while we hoped and prayed at every scan that there was no sign of hydrops.

But what we weren't prepared for was 3 years of unexplained infertility, being told our only option was ivf, and then immediately conceiving, the highs and lows were beyond anything we could've imagined.

We weren't prepared for the 2 missed miscarriages and 2 lots of surgery my body would have to endure within 5 months.... none of that was part of our grand plan to extend our family.

However, going through all that really had made us stronger, and much closer, of course it had been tough, there had been many low points, and after all we went through, I honestly thought we should give up, that there was no way we were ever going to get the baby we had wanted for such a long time. I began to move forward, got a new job, and began to look to the future with the beautiful little family we already had.

Fast forward 6 months from that point I had just dropped my boys off at school overly excited to tell all their friends that they were going to be big brothers.... yes, that's right, we made it to 12 weeks pregnant with what can only be described as our little miracle. 3 happy, healthy scans down the line we couldn't keep it from the kids for any longer and they were elated!

I had decided there wasn't going to be any big announcement, I still wasn't confident that things would be ok, but I just couldn't really hide it anymore. Pregnancy was never going to be easy for us, and it certainly wasn't all excitement and baby catalogues in my head, but we just had to hope and pray that this really was our time.

I went back to work finally at 13 weeks pregnant when the sickness had started to ease, but lasted only 2 days, horrendous labour type pains had me up all night and had us expecting the worst, numerous (completely pointless) phone calls to our (completely awful and incredibly rude) early pregnancy unit, both in the middle of the night and the next morning got us nowhere, so I took a trip to my GP instead.

GP was luckily lovely, and my sister stamped her feet a bit and complained about the awful people at EPU resulting in the GP ringing them herself and getting them to bring my scan forward to that afternoon.

It was an incredibly stressful 24 hours to say the least.... however, the scan showed a happy healthy 13-week pregnancy, though gave us no ideas as to where the pain came from, but 13 weeks!!! We made it!

We were now officially on to the next hurdle.... the 50/50 chance of hydrops to contend with now.... BUT we had proved we can survive anything thrown at us so far, so surely, we could do this too?

EIGHTEEN

In some ways I missed the naivety of first pregnancy, I remember all those years ago after my first scan, the excitement and the need to go shopping at every opportunity, sadly my experiences since then had taken that away, pregnancy for me now was all about getting through each week, each appointment, each scan, and I knew until at least 30 weeks – when my baby girl was diagnosed – (to be fair probably even longer than that) I wouldn't be able to feel any of that excitement, only fear and nervous anticipation…. but I guess only people who have experienced baby loss will truly understand that, and I'm glad in a way, because I wouldn't wish that feeling on anybody else.

Of course, it's not right to say I wasn't excited, this baby meant the world to us and of course I was happy, but I also had this inbuilt defence mechanism to shield myself from any unnecessary pain. So, I won't apologise for not broadcasting our happy news for the whole world to see.

I also won't apologise for not posting happy pictures of our children holding our scan pictures, or pictures of my expanding belly…. it's not that I didn't take them, of course I did, and I definitely don't disagree with other people doing the same, in fact quite the opposite, I loved seeing other people's happy family posts they always made me smile…. once upon a time I was the same, but these days these things were precious to us as a family, I was well aware of the chance that one day these things may be all we had…. so, for that reason they stayed between the closest people to us.

Sadly, my boys understood that there was a chance this baby might be poorly…. we talked about it a little as I'd much rather be honest with them right from the start, they were SO excited (we had frequent shopping trip suggestions!) and their excitement helped me to feel excitement too.

We had told them they had to wait until a few weeks before baby was born before we could buy anything, but we had a lot more reasoning to do with them!

At 14 weeks pregnant we received the news that I was carrying group B strep... just one more thing to stress about (and wish I hadn't googled.... I'll learn one day!!) and I also had a conversation with our lovely genetics doctor in London, who confirmed that the chances of this baby developing hydrops were indeed around 50% as we had thought.

On top of that was a particularly long and stressful phone call trying to bring forward a consultant's appointment, trying to explain to the incredibly useless receptionist that 24 weeks REALLY WAS too late for my first appointment regardless of what her bloody traffic light system said was bloody hard work and very emotional, but luckily a lovely midwife sorted it out for me.

The positives of the week were making it back to work – the distraction and purpose was exactly what I needed, and I also managed to take smallest boy to his swimming lesson – this may seem mundane and not worth writing about, however in my world it was a massive achievement. I had felt so incredibly guilty every Wednesday for weeks that he had missed his lesson, not only that, but he's missed that precious one to one time with his mummy whilst we chatted for half an hour each way.... but I REALLY hadn't felt well enough to take him, the last time we went I had to sit outside for his whole lesson as I felt so sick and faint, he cried because I hadn't seen his "epic dive" and I have absolutely no idea how I made it home in one piece!

So, the smallest of things, the tiniest of achievements was pretty big in that moment. It felt like I had turned a corner; the sickness seemed to have passed (until around 5-6pm anyway and I could cope with that!) I had managed to go to work and besides having a headache EVERY bloody afternoon forcing me into bed by the time smallest boy was in his pyjamas I was surviving much better than I had in months.

Surviving.... some might say that's not the way to describe pregnancy, many say it's a period to relish, to enjoy, and of course, I was happy to be pregnant, and of course I understood there are so many people out there who would do ANYTHING to be pregnant right now, I had been in their shoes, I had battled infertility, and multiple miscarriages, I knew exactly how it felt. But I was also experiencing pregnancy after loss, both after miscarriage and neonatal death, and believe me pregnancy after baby loss was most definitely all about survival.

One day at a time was possibly the only way to survive.... each appointment became a milestone that needed to be overcome.

Somehow, in a bit of a blur we arrived at the anniversary of my second miscarriage, it was a weird feeling, in some ways it felt like it happened just yesterday, in other ways it could've been 10 years.

Anniversaries are always tough, but this one was a particularly shit day. However, I ended the day at my monthly WI meeting, I hadn't made it for a few months as I had been feeling so rubbish, but it turned out to be just what I needed, we watched (and learned) burlesque and laughed A LOT! I can safely say I'll probably never ever do it again, but it was incredibly fun and brightened up a rubbish day!

It was difficult to believe what my body had been through over the course of a year, recovering from my first miscarriage was incredibly tough, it then experienced 12 weeks of pregnancy before another miscarriage and more surgery, and although thankfully much less traumatic and with a much quicker recovery it was still a lot to deal with. But 1 year down the line and 15 weeks pregnant, every part of me was just hoping and praying that I NEVER had to step foot in that awful early pregnancy unit again, (I'm sure all the people that have accompanied me there will agree!) and that we would make it until December.

Pregnancy after loss was a massive journey, full of so many highs and lows and it was bloody exhausting, adding anniversaries into the mix just seemed like a special kind of torture... But I was determined that I would not only survive it, but that I would come out the other side smiling.

NINETEEN

At 16 weeks pregnant we got to see our baby again, for hubby's birthday present we went for a reassurance scan and got to see our baby in 4d.

I was terrified, and ready to leave before we'd even gone in, But the sonographer was lovely, within 30 seconds she'd shown us our happy healthy kicking baby, we watched it sucking its thumb and waving its hand and we came away with lots of pictures and a feeling that it's all much more real, a little reassurance can go an awfully long way.

We went out for some food afterwards and even braved a trip to the shops (not that we bought anything, but we picked up catalogues and let ourselves dream and make plans for a little while), it was nice to act like any other expectant parents even if just for a moment, some positive thinking was good for us both.

It was beginning to feel like we might really get to meet this baby, I spent the evening packing away all my clothes that no longer fitted into bags under the bed and replaced them with maternity clothes given to me by a lovely friend. I was finally feeling human again too, the sickness had completely gone, and dizziness much better, headaches were much less often, and I felt surprisingly good, the second trimester was obviously agreeing with me MUCH better than the first!

In other news.... we got a little teddy bear with a recording of baby's heartbeat inside from our scan, we let littlest boy name the teddy Tim, and in return he agreed to let me, and daddy name the baby – id say that was a parenting win in itself!

At 19 weeks, I cried publicly through my biggest boys' entire leavers service, cried reading his guitar and keyboard lesson reports, and cried because I was running out of satsumas!

I DO NOT cry in public... EVER.

In fact, even my closest friends were surprised by my tears, therefore I blamed hormones for all the above!

By my 20th week, I could feel baby moving and kicking which helped to lessen my worrying. The day hubby felt it for the first time he had tears in his eyes, then when smallest boy did, he was SO excited I thought he might burst, he had to ring daddy to tell him too it was incredibly cute and made me realize just how lucky I was.

I had spent several weeks worrying before my first consultant appointment, in fact at 2am one morning I was up writing a list of all the things I needed to say, all the things I needed to make sure were put in place, and I had psyched myself up for stamping my feet until they agreed to follow the same level of care I had in my last pregnancy.... I was even ready to transfer my care over to the hospital my other children were born at if they did not agree to monitor baby closely enough.

The fact I had waited for so long to get a consultant appointment did not help, my midwife was adamant I should've been seen weeks earlier, and I was on the verge of transferring my care to the more specialist hospital that was further away – even though I had been adamant from the very start that I wanted this time to be different, to be closer to home.

Eventually though, it appeared that all my worrying had been for nothing, in fact after my appointment, all my faith in my local hospital had been restored completely (after such awful experiences in their early pregnancy unit last year, coupled with my pretty traumatic experience when finding out my daughters' problems there all those years ago I had little faith)

I saw the loveliest doctor -sadly, he was not my consultant – he was covering as she was on annual leave – but, he had read my notes BEFORE I went in, he asked questions about my daughter, about the care I had received, about the outcomes of all my pregnancies, and all the interventions that I had had previously. He seemed to genuinely care.

I did not have to ask for anything at all, I did not need my list, or to make myself heard, he asked how I had been looked after in previous pregnancies, how often I had been monitored and scanned etc and he arranged for MORE monitoring in this pregnancy, he told me he wanted me to have no reason at all to be any more anxious than I had cause to be.

So, I had a plan! Scans and consultant appointments every 2 weeks from 24 weeks…. and I was told I could go in ANYTIME I had any concerns at all, and then he even went to see another consultant to check if there was anything else they could do for me…and there was me all geared up for an argument!!

I left feeling so much more positive than I had done in a long time, and so happy I stuck with what I wanted, to be as close to home as possible. Now we just needed all the scans to go well…

Only a few days later I returned to the hospital for my 20-week anomaly scan.

I was incredibly stressed and incredibly worried, and it was a VERY long half an hour lying there being scanned waiting to hear that everything was ok.

The anxiety was made even worse by spending at least half of that time with the bed tipped upside down as baby was in an awkward position!

HOWEVER, baby looked perfect.... no sign of smallest man's kidney problem (which we had been given a 25% chance of recurring) and more importantly no sign of hydrops, so far so good!

We had the same lovely sonographer as our 13-week scan and he could not have been nicer, even after he had finished, he went back and rechecked baby's fluid to reassure us there were no signs of hydrops, we could not have had better care.

Another consultant appointment followed – this time a different Dr who just agreed with the plan that was made the previous week. In fact, it took far longer to book my next 7 scan appointments and consultant appointments than the actual appointment itself.

Afterwards we braved some window shopping and picked out some baby things that we liked, another tiny hint of normality whilst the positivity of a good scan lasted, going home to compile a list of things to be bought at some point further down the line.

I spent most of the next day feeling guilty for the lack of excitement.... longing for the days before pregnancy loss when I would have been bursting with excitement and shopping for so many gorgeous baby items. I was tired and grumpy for most of the day, although hubby did eventually convince me to take the boys out and we enjoyed a lovely evening at the park with them having lots of fun together.

It seemed like my life was now all about desperately trying to hold onto the hope that the scan had brought us to get us through until the next one, these next few weeks were going to be the most crucial…. hydrops developed between 20-30 weeks in my first 2 pregnancies, so we were now in the "danger zone". I needed to try and stay busy and stay positive, but some days that was easier said than done.

My nights had been full of crazy vivid dreams too…. waking me up several times a night which I guess did not help my mood much…. especially when they felt so real.

By this point my bump was VERY obvious, which meant the unwanted comments had begun. and I have to say that although most were well meaning, and most people were kind, some of the, just really pissed me off!

"I bet you're praying this one's a girl?" (which I had more times than I can count)

"This one will definitely be a girl; you must want a daughter."

"Ooh starting all over again when the boys are big and independent."

"Oh no you can't have 3, 3 is a bad number."

And my favorite one of all…

"God, was it planned?!" In a shocked, horrified voice.

I thought at first that I was tired and hormonal and maybe overreacting, but the more I thought about it, seriously?

what the actual fuck??

Just in case anyone was wondering, no we were not praying for a girl.... We were praying for a healthy baby.

I already had a daughter, and so did my hubby. None of us could care in the slightest the sex of our baby, and he/she being healthy really was all that we were hoping for.

Secondly, yes, we were starting all over again, smallest boy was 7. But no, it is not how we planned it, we planned it 4 whole years earlier!

But would we change it? No, not at all.

Thirdly, this was not child number 3 in any sense.... this was my 4th baby.... it also would not be the 3rd living child in our family.... my 2 boys and my stepdaughter already made 3!

And finally, yes it was planned, very much so, not that our sex life should be anyone else's business!!

I would not ever even dream of saying any of those things to another woman so I struggle to comprehend why anyone else would say them to me....

Yet I continued to smile, nod and ignore people's comments, concentrate on the amazing life growing inside me, and the amazing little family we already had.

Interfering people may feel free to comment on my beautiful family, our choices and our lives but at the end of the day we were entitled to ignore them, and so, we did.

TWENTY

The third trimester was upon us, and our 24-week scan could not have gone better, another lovely sonographer who had a thorough look at baby at declared it to be hydrops free.

The relief in the room was immense!

The 2 hour wait to see my consultant afterwards was not so fun, however once I did get in there it was quite productive, she told me that there was another consultant at the hospital who specialized in fetal medicine, so she wanted to transfer my care to him as she felt he was better equipped to look after me and do more detailed scans etc. So, as much of a pain as it was changing all my appointments and hubby changing all the days he had booked off work, we decided it was a positive step, being kept a closer eye on could only be a good thing!

High on positivity, we even managed a little shopping trip after the hospital to buy baby their first teddy and pick up a few hospital bag things, they were then very quickly and safely hidden out of my sight to save me feeling like I had tempted fate.

I had decided that now we had reached 24 weeks, this baby was going to be born and whatever the outcome, it would need some items of its own - though that really didn't help the feeling of dread that came over me once I had bought them.

As the days passed slowly waiting for my next scan my positivity was very quickly disappearing. I had reached the point in pregnancy where my biggest boy was diagnosed with hydrops now, and to say I was terrified would be an understatement.

The big boys had gone back to school after the summer holidays – with smallest boy going into the juniors and biggest boy starting high school – massive changes for them both and a rollercoaster of emotions for me! I had also returned to work after the summer, which was helping to keep my mind busy.

I thought I was doing well, in fact since the last scan me and hubby had done lots of decision making, list writing and even bought of few bits for baby.

It may sound morbid, and I am guessing only those who have been through baby loss will get this, but my thinking had changed from "we won't get to meet this baby" to "this baby is going to be born now, they will need certain things regardless of whether they live or die".

I had reasoned with myself about this so many times, and this was the only thought process stopping the guilt at buying stuff some days.

Don't get me wrong, on other days (especially the first few days following the last scan) positivity was high, and there was huge excitement involved in choosing gorgeous things for our baby to wear etc., but on those dark days waiting for the next appointment, where sleep was not my friend and there were too many "what ifs" in my head the thoughts of losing this baby consumed me.

A random person commented how big I was for 26 weeks

pregnant and how I must've been going to have a huge baby this time. I managed to smile and nod, then rant about it later. Luckily, I had reached a point in my journey where other people's comments could mainly just go straight over my head, I could file them away as well-meaning as I knew for those who did not know my journey or had not experienced loss would have no idea the effect their comments could have.

That is one thing that loss has taught me, to NEVER comment on a woman's body, pregnancy or fertility unless invited to!

Measuring too big was the first sign of hydrops with my precious girl, and biggest boy, so any comments about my size – however innocent or well meaning – generally made me want to run away and hide.

The day before our 26 week scan a parcel arrived, some things we had ordered in our excitement just 2 weeks earlier, and now the guilt I felt about tempting fate was immense. I really couldn't win, a few weeks earlier I had felt guilty for not being excited enough and not having bought anything for baby, so we made the huge decision to start buying a few bits – though we were still not letting anybody else – and now I felt guilty because we got over excited and ordered some.

I guess there really was no right or wrong solution to this, whatever we did I was going to feel bad, feel guilty... pregnancy after loss does strange things to your thinking.

We did it though, we passed the 26-week scan with no sign of hydrops! Passed the point biggest boy was diagnosed, the scan was perfect, sonographer was lovely, and baby cooperated without me having to be tipped upside down! Baby had turned over and was now breech and kicking away happily.

I also met my new consultant who basically just agreed with the plan we already had in place, booked some more scans and said, "see you in 2 weeks". We relished in the short and simple appointment, celebrated by going shopping for some glamourous things like breast pads for my hospital bag!

28 weeks came around quickly, and in a way, I wanted to jump up and down for joy as there was still no sign of hydrops, which at that stage was incredible news, however, it wasn't all plain sailing this time.

We arrived at the ultrasound department and after a short wait were called in, I was being scanned by a consultant this time, and she was lovely. She was quick to reassure us that there was no sign of hydrops, and she took all the measurements etc., baby was not cooperating very well so we could not get a picture, but we came out of the room feeling ecstatic that everything was going well.

My mum had come with us to the scan, and she left at this point to get to work whilst me and hubby went back to the waiting room whilst the consultant wrote the scan report. After about 5 minutes she came back and called me – we presumed to give me back my notes – but instead she told me that I needed to be rescanned as the measurements were showing something wrong.

I can't even describe what was going through my head at this point as we went into another scan room to start again.

This time was much quicker, and the wait afterwards also much quicker, when she came back, she explained that baby had dropped down on its growth chart, that 2 weeks ago it had been measuring in the 15th centile but now it was only on the 10th centile, and the very bottom of the chart. She explained how important it was that I keep a close eye on movements etc and sent me round to see my consultant.

My consultant basically said the same thing, that baby's growth needed monitoring closely and I would need growth scans every 2 weeks, though we already had scans booked to check for hydrops every 2 weeks, so basically, we went in worrying that baby and fluid would be measuring too big.... and came out worrying that it is measuring too small!

So now, although celebrating that there was no hydrops, we were anxious.

Pregnancy is not meant to be easy right?!

TWENTY ONE

Baby loss awareness week happens every October, ending in a global wave of light on baby loss awareness day.

This year, at 29 weeks pregnant and terrified of what was to come, I was more emotional than in previous years and I struggled with myself deciding whether to go to the annual remembrance service at my local church. I was conscious that my huge bump may be difficult for some people early on in their baby loss journeys to see, but hubby convinced me that I would regret it if I stayed at home.

Smallest boy made me very proud though, when we arrived he wrote in his neatest handwriting 3 name cards to be read out in the service, one for his big sister, and 1 each for "our two babies that died in your tummy", he made a point of collecting 3 flowers when they were passed around so that they all had one each, he collected 3 candles to light to remember them all, and he took his sharpie collection in his pocket so that he could write them all their own balloons and draw them all their own picture for the balloon release at the end.

A lot of tears were shed that afternoon, probably more than in previous years, I am blaming hormones for many of them, but one thing remains, being in that enormous church, FULL of other people who have experienced baby loss, listening to the hundreds of baby names being read out, watching countless other families release their balloons for their precious babies made me realise every single year just how many people are affected by baby loss, just in my local area.

Our little rainbow kicked the whole way through the service, giving me a shred of hope through the darkness, and being a part of the service just proved how much it mattered to me and made me more and more determined to carry on going, to keep telling my story and sharing my journey in the hope that it may bring a small amount of comfort or hope to somebody else.

Baby loss really is shit.

Miscarriage really is shit.

Infertility really is shit.

Pregnancy after loss is terrifying.

But all these things happen so much more often than anyone would think, and we need to talk about them more, we need people to know they are not alone, we need to break down the taboos. To allow women (and their partners/families) to be heard, to feel cared for, to have their feelings validated rather than ignored.

TWENTY TWO

With only 3 days until our next scan, I had been doing particularly well.

Me and hubby had sorted through the baby stuff we had bought to try and find it all a home, but I then spent that night in and out of sleep having awful dreams. Some about being sent to a quiet room after our scan to receive bad news, the rest about having to return all the stuff we had cautiously bought because we would not get to bring this baby home after all.

I should have been proud of myself for being brave and trying to be a "normal excited pregnant person" instead I was exhausted and feeling guilty for tempting fate.

30 weeks is the point they found hydrops in my first pregnancy, so I saw this scan as the last big milestone to get through, but on top of the hydrops, I was now also anxious that baby had grown enough after they were so concerned last time.

The good news was that the scan once again showed no hydrops. We had finally passed that last big milestone that had been playing on my mind.

30 weeks and 3 days was the exact day in which my beautiful girl was diagnosed with hydrops – even though in hindsight she'd probably had it for quite some time by then – so seeing our little rainbow fluid free at that exact same gestation was amazing, and it felt (briefly) like we were doing good, that the "highest risk period" was over.

At that point, in my happy state I even excused the rude sonographer, who hadn't bothered to look at my notes before we had gone in, so she had to ask me why I was there and why I was having extra scans.... this SERIOUSLY annoyed me more than it should, but the happiness of being hydrops free meant I didn't let it get to me as much as normal.

After the scan we went back to the waiting room again while she did the scan report and after what seemed like forever, she called us back to explain that baby's growth had once again dropped and it was now measuring below the 10th centile.

That joy had been short lived, and as we walked down the corridor to the antenatal clinic all I felt was fear.

I saw a lovely midwife then waited for a Dr, and after seeing the scan report there was a bit of debate between the Dr and consultant as to whether to give me steroid injections immediately in order to prepare for early delivery. Eventually they decided to give baby 2 weeks to "catch up" because the Doppler on the placenta was fine and baby was active.

So, the plan was to monitor movements closely for the next 2 weeks and if baby hadn't moved back to at least the 10th centile by the next scan then then they would give me steroids that day and discuss delivering that week.

I was terrified.

32 weeks was far too early, the journey to our happy ever after was worse than any rollercoaster.

The highs and lows were off the scale.

We always knew this pregnancy was going to be tough, we just hadn't anticipated it being in a completely different way to the others.

Somehow, I still felt lucky, I had my amazing hubby, family and some incredibly supportive friends around me and the Drs were doing all they could to keep this baby safe.

But I was exhausted by it all, and keeping a brave face was getting progressively harder.

The next 2 weeks passed incredibly slowly once more, but we finally arrived at the hospital, perhaps more nervous than ever, and the scan was amazing!

Not only did we have the loveliest sonographer ever, we got to watch baby sucking its thumb, and see that it already had a head full of hair, but most importantly it showed that baby had grown enough and had moved back up to the 10th centile and so could stay inside for another few weeks.... woo hoo!!

The consultant appointment that followed went pretty smoothly, but led to me needing to take iron supplements, to be booked in for a glucose tolerance test, and a decision that they wanted to deliver at 38 weeks.... It was all a bit too much to take in if I'm honest...

Nesting had reached spectacular heights by now, (even hubby had joined in and been on all fours with a scrubbing brush on the bathroom floor) our house was gleaming, and the freezer was full of healthy meals that I had made and frozen for when the time came.

We had even sorted out some drawers for baby and bought

almost everything we needed for the first couple of weeks, all that was left to do was to buy some little newborn vests and sleepsuits and pack a bag!

TWENTY THREE

I finished work at 33 weeks pregnant, and although thankful of the break I was bored! There was only so much tv I could watch, and only so much crochet I could do. Now I was much less worried about baby my mind was much less occupied than it had been over the past 7 months, and of course that wasn't a bad thing, but it did mean that I needed more entertaining, being alone with my thoughts all day was not doing me any good at all.

I decided to ease the boredom and keep me busy, that I would sort Christmas, to get everything bought, wrapped and be done and sorted so that once baby arrived, I didn't have to even think about it. I even found the courage to order a few presents for baby, and although they stayed hidden away in their packaging, I was still proud of myself for allowing that positivity and planning to happen.

Me and hubby went along to a breastfeeding information evening at our local hospital and although I didn't personally learn very much – probably because I'd spent all morning reading a book given to me by a lovely friend – it was still good to be there, see how much support there was in my local area, and hubby came away having learnt loads and feeling even more certain that we had made the right decision for our baby and our family.

I never would have thought that I would be brave enough to go to a group like that, and I am not going to lie I was nervous. Since losing my baby girl I could not stand group situations like that, the awkward questions of how many children I have etc., especially in a group of mainly first-time mums, so before we arrived me and hubby decided we would just not get into that.

When the leader assumed that everybody there were first time parents, we did not correct her (until the end when we spoke to her in private). It's not that I didn't want to talk about my children – quite the opposite – I just didn't want to be that person scaring all the pregnant women with her horror stories – I didn't want to be that woman whose baby died that no one wants to sit next to…. sometimes it was simply better to sit quietly and not comment.

The next day was my glucose tolerance test. I started the day in a rubbish mood, having been allowed nothing but water since 10pm the night before, I got up early and was starving!

I sat through breakfast with my boys almost resenting their every mouthful, dropped smallest boy with my sister so she could take him to school and walked down to the hospital. By the time I got there I was already shattered and had to sit and wait for half an hour for my turn. The midwife was lovely, she took my blood and explained what would happen, then handed me a plastic cup full of "glucose solution" to drink.

Anyone that knows me well knows how fussy I am and what a wimp I am, but seriously the stuff was DISGUSTING.

Thick and gloopy orange liquid that I had to force down, that made me heave. It took me nearly 10 minutes to drink the vile stuff, by which point I could have cried!

It is a good job I had a patient midwife who told me she cared more that it stayed down, and I could sit there all day drinking it if I needed too – I'm not sure she realised that that was a distinct possibility!

After I had finally finished, I had to sit back in the hot busy waiting room for 2 hours whilst I waited for my next blood test which wasn't much fun, but it was soon over, and I got to go home and wait for the results.

I laughed to myself when I got home, after all that I had been through in the past few years, out of all the procedures and stress I had been through in my journey so far, I would never have imagined that drinking a drink would be high up there on my worst experiences list!

Only a couple of days later, an 8am phone call from the hospital telling me I had gestational diabetes was not what I either wanted or expected.

I spent 2 hours flitting between tears and anger at my body for once again not being able to do things right, terrified of what was to come with no idea what the implications were for both me and my baby.

I was given an appointment for a few days later to see the diabetes specialist midwife and told I would be given a blood sugar monitor and be taught how to use it etc. and told that in the meantime I must try and change my diet to get my blood sugar under control.

I cried so much that day. Seriously wondering what on earth I had done to deserve all this and wondering how much more strength I could find to deal with everything that was being thrown at me.

We had come SO far; but it seemed that every time we got a glimmer of hope something else popped up out of nowhere to bring us crashing back down.

After an incredibly stressful weekend trying to come to terms with having yet another problem to overcome our next scan brought the good news we needed.

Baby had grown exactly along the 10th centile, so not only were there no worries about it not growing, but it also meant that my newly diagnosed gestational diabetes had not affected baby by making growth too fast which was the latest concern – even I couldn't keep up by now, but we all breathed a huge sigh of relief.

After a lot of discussion about who needed to lead my care now my health had changed, it was decided that it was more important that the fetal medicine specialist consultant continued my care rather than transferring me to the diabetes consultant, as they were confident that I could control my blood sugars without the need for medication.

Plans had to change as they no longer wanted to give me steroids and bring baby out at 38 weeks due to the risks to my blood sugar levels from the steroids, so I was told to work hard to keep my levels under control and hope that baby continued to grow along the same line at the next scan in 2 weeks' time which would mean delivery could be at 39 weeks instead and eliminate the need for steroids.

After all this we saw the diabetes specialist midwife, she gave me my blood glucose monitor, needles and test strips etc and showed me how to use them. It was all a lot to take in to be fair, I was awfully glad hubby was with me to ask questions and remember things. I spent the next few days very frustrated making several failed attempts at getting enough blood to even test, stressing about trying to change needles, and overall. feeling like a bit of a failure.

After a few days of trial and error I did eventually figure it out. There was still so much to learn, and so many questions to ask, but I seemed to have got my head round the whole diabetes thing much quicker than I thought I would, I had changed my diet so much that my levels had all been ok, I gave up sugar completely and can honestly say I didn't even miss it. Keeping my baby safe had given me the motivation I needed.

Time seemed to be going SO slowly now though, every day felt like a week, I wasn't sleeping very well so was exhausted most of the time, it seemed my body was preparing me for life with a newborn... I still wasn't sure I believed that might be about to happen?!

The end of this part of our journey was nearly in sight. It had been one hell of a ride, but I knew it would all be worth it soon enough.

By 36 weeks I was exhausted and hungry!

My new diet to control my diabetes was becoming increasingly difficult for someone as fussy as me, as most foods I would normally eat were now either completely off limits or rationed, and although the diabetes consultant being incredibly pleased with how well I was doing did make it all seem much more worthwhile, knowing I was doing everything I could to protect this baby, it sadly didn't stop it being really fucking hard.

I was becoming increasingly bored and fed up, I had a huge list of jobs that needed doing before baby arrived, but most of them I just couldn't physically do myself, and with hubby at work every day doing 12 hour shifts there just weren't enough hours in the day for him to get stuff done at home too.

Luckily, the boys were being incredibly helpful and helping me out lots round the house, but it was just SO frustrating not being able to get stuff done myself!

I was so sick of sitting in the house all day looking at all the things that needed doing, but then I was too exhausted to do much else. My very restricted diet meant I couldn't even go for a trip to the local coffee shop as there was nothing there that I could (or would) eat or drink.

It was just another scenario where I just couldn't win.... I felt guilty for not enjoying the last few weeks of pregnancy, after all I knew I was never going to be doing this again, and I felt guilty for not making the most of every single moment with my boys before their new sibling arrived and life became even more chaotic.

I felt guilty every single time I moaned, and every time I got annoyed with someone's stupid comment.

I really would not have changed any of this for anything in the world. This pregnancy, this baby was all we had hoped for the past 4 and a half years, and the journey we'd been on to get this far had been hell.

I really was thankful for every single second of this pregnancy, for every single kick, every minute of lost sleep, and every single worry I had about this baby.

We really had given up hope of ever getting this far.

Our final scan at 36 weeks showed that my diabetes had started to affect baby's growth.

It had gone from measuring on the 10th centile to its stomach now measuring on the 100th centile.

The baby they had been so worried about not growing enough was now growing too much.

I really struggled to get my head round this as I had stuck so meticulously to my diet and tried SO incredibly hard to keep this baby safe and not let my sugar levels affect it, and even though I had managed to keep all my levels within target baby had still been affected.

My final consultant appointment led to a decision to deliver at 38 weeks, and the need for steroid injections first to give baby the best chance at not needing any special care, so I was booked for a weekend stay in hospital so that I could have the injections and they could monitor my blood sugars closely/treat me with insulin if required.

When I arrived at the hospital with my suitcase, I was told that I didnt need to stay in, that if I monitored by blood sugar closely, I could go home again and return only if my levels became too high. I was thankful to spend that weekend with my boys. I was tired, anxious, and even bordering occasionally on excited!

With only a couple of days to go now sleep deserted me, the only job really left to do was to wash baby clothes.... a job that had been put off for so long in fear of tempting fate.... but I finally braved taking them out of the packets and getting them ready to be washed and packed in my bag.

It still didn't feel real that very soon, in only a couple of days' time in fact, they would be worn by our baby.

TWENTY FOUR

Finally, birth day arrived, and thankfully it was far less stressful than I'd imagined.

We arrived on delivery suite early in the morning, nervous yet excited, we were told there was an emergency before us, but we should still be in theatre by 9.30.... I was in my gown and stockings by 8.15am and had seen both the consultant and anaesthetist by 9am. It couldn't have gone any better.

Then the waiting began!

By 1pm nerves were starting to set in, I'd been calm up to this point, but a midwife came to see me and told me that they were just handing over to the next shift then I'd be taken straight to theatre.

This was really happening!

Half an hour passed by and the midwife came back, this time to explain that there was a problem with the heating in theatre and they had had to wait for an engineer to come and turn it up. This amused us more than it should've done, that there was a theatre full of all these highly qualified people and no one could work the heating - I think the laughter and ridiculous thought of it kept us sane in those moments.

Before we knew it, we were being taken round to the (still rather cold!) theatre.

All the staff in there were lovely, we chatted away whilst they got everything set up, and they sang along to Christmas songs on the radio!

Hubby came in a few minutes later as they were ready to do my spinal anaesthetic, he then took selfies of him watching me have it done to amuse himself whilst I was trying to keep very still!

The atmosphere in the room was amazing, we chatted and laughed, me still not quite believing what was happening.

I remember saying to hubby even as I lay there being cut open that it still didn't feel real, that they could actually be doing anything to me, at that point I still didn't actually believe that I was going to have a baby!

Just seconds after that hubby stood up, he looked over the screen and watched as the surgeons lifted our gorgeous baby boy out of me, he was screaming before his legs were even out, and I sobbed and sobbed as the realisation set in.

He was quickly dried off and put onto my chest, and immediately I fell in love with our tiny, perfect little man. He latched on and breastfed almost immediately, something I'd really wanted to do but wasn't sure if I'd manage, I was elated.

His big brothers and sister came to meet him a few hours later, and they were (luckily) all incredibly happy to find out that he was a boy!

He passed all his observations within 12 hours, I passed my final blood sugar check, and we were both discharged healthy and happy within 24 hours of him being born, and although sore from the surgery, and incredibly tired things couldn't have been more perfect.

I had a bit of a wobble when the midwife visited when he was a couple of days old and asked if I'd had an appointment for his tongue tie referral, something I wasn't even aware he had, I spent hours searching the internet for information and was a bit bombarded and slightly terrified.

We went on our first trip out when he was just 6 days old to his brothers Christmas carol service in church, and I breastfed in public for the very first time, something I wasn't particularly confident about – but we did it, and it really wasn't at all traumatic, in fact that was far less traumatic than the projectile poo he did all over his pram at the end of the service!

Once he was 10 days old, I spent the entire night lay wide awake worrying, baby had been weighed the day before and he had lost weight, he also had jaundice despite him seeming to be feeding really well. I was devastated. Mummy guilt kicked in and I spent hours online reading.

I had really thought that things were going well, and that breastfeeding was the one thing that I could get right. But the midwife had told us we had only 3 days until the next weigh in for him to put weight on before I would have to give him formula and I was beyond upset.

We tried expressing milk and cup feeding him after his feeds, but soon realised that his tongue tie meant he couldn't actually move his tongue to drink from the cup, so against the advice from the midwife we resorted to syringe feeding instead.

I was desperate to avoid formula. Desperate to be able to exclusively breastfeed, it was so important to me that my broken body could at least do that.

Motherhood is not meant to be easy, I had to keep reminding myself of that, the early newborn days were supposed to be a rollercoaster, after all we had just entered a new chapter and we had a lot to learn.

Despite the stress and the anxiety, it was all worth it, every sleepless night, every moment spent worrying, every single tear that was shed.

Every single thing we had to go through, I'd do it all a million times over, we had our happy ending, our gorgeous rainbow baby in our arms. Every obstacle we came across now was nothing compared to what it took to get him here, and I wouldn't be a Mum if I didn't spend my whole life worrying about something!

TWENTY FIVE

By the time he was 2 weeks old it seemed like he had been here forever, being pregnant was a distant memory, all the heartache had literally just erased from my memory, filed away and replaced by this huge, overwhelming love for our little family.

Christmas was manic as usual, but lovely at the same time, all of our children and nieces together having fun, noisy, crazy, just how Christmas should be.... that's not to say it wasn't exhausting though!

The midwife returned and little man had not only got rid of his jaundice completely, but he had also actually put some weight on too... thank goodness!

He still wasn't back to his birth weight, so we still had to keep a close eye on him and reweigh him again in another week, BUT he was going in the right direction. We were winning the breastfeeding battle and I was pretty proud of myself for not giving up. His tongue tie referral had finally been made too so everything was looking good.

All of this coincided with hubbys first day back at work, I had spent the day alone with all 4 children, and we had all survived! In fact, we'd done better than survived.... Everyone had been washed, dressed and fed, I had a load of washing in and had washed the pots, we managed a trip to the Drs (thanks to my sister having 2 of them to save me too much trauma!!) and a trip to the park (I did forget to sort anything for tea but I'm ignoring that minor detail!)

I felt like I was winning at life, we spent the evening with a lovely roast dinner, playing board games and eating chocolate, with our smallest boy cluster feeding throughout the entire night, permanently attached to my breast.

I honestly didn't think life could be any more perfect.

It was strange to think that 2017 was almost over. We had started the year so low after suffering our second miscarriage only a few weeks earlier and having all but given up on our dream of extending our family after 4 years of heartache. It had been a year full of ups and downs, there had been so many moments when we didn't think we would make it, so many tough times.... But now our beautiful rainbow was here safe and sound, all the hard times and tough moments had paled into insignificance, we were ending the year the happiest (and tiredest!!) we had ever been, surrounded by our beautiful little family, and our big crazy family too.

Not only was the year over, but our journey to complete our family was over too. We would be starting the new year with everything we had wanted for such a very long time, with our family finally complete, starting the next step of our journey through life. Determined to make the most of every single moment, to cherish every "first" and every "last" and to create even more happy memories.

The boys soon went back to school after the holidays, and it was just me and our smallest boy for the first time. On our first day flying solo, the health visitor came to weigh little man and found he'd finally got back up to (and past) his birth weight, I was a VERY relieved mummy at that point!

That afternoon we went for a trip to see the infant feeding team at our local hospital about his tongue tie, the lady was SO lovely, and made me feel like I was actually doing things right, immediately after looking at him she said it definitely needed cutting, it was 75% tied and she went to make some calls to get him booked in asap.

She managed to book him in the very next day and it went so much better than I thought it would and was over very quickly, although he cried a lot it was nowhere near as traumatic as I had imagined. In fact, little man fed immediately afterwards and then slept the whole way home!

TWENTY SIX

By the time smallest boy was a month old I was consciously trying to enjoy every moment, trying not to wish the time away and was just so overwhelmed with love and happiness. Everything was SO different this time around, I was running on very little sleep, but love (and chocolate) was getting me through in my little bubble of happiness.

I was now so incredibly glad of the big age gap between our children, although our journey had been long and tough, I was verging on being grateful for it! The timing couldn't have been more right for us as a family.

I was older and far more confident this time around, (probably thanks to everything I went through in the early days of both bigger boys and in our journey this time around) but it had made sure I was far more confident in my own abilities, and in myself, and happy in making parenting decisions.

The big boys were incredible with their baby brother, they adored him, couldn't wait to give him a cuddle as soon as they got up in the mornings, and as soon as they got home from school. They suddenly seemed even more grown up, and I marvelled at what lovely boys they were growing into.

I can honestly say that even though breastfeeding had been more stressful at first than I had hoped, it was still the one thing I was most proud of, thanks to the support of my hubby and some fab friends I amazed even myself at how easy it was and how confident I was.

I had thought I'd be embarrassed and hide away in the house, but my mother's instinct took over and upon little man requiring a feed all embarrassment immediately evaporated and the need to calm my baby took over. Even in just the first month I had already found myself feeding him in shops, in church and even on park benches without a care in the world!

I had a newfound confidence, coupled with the amazing bond I felt, sitting cuddled up together whilst he fed with him staring up at me has got to be the best feeling in the world.

A whole month had passed since my Caesarean and I felt like it could've been years ago, everything had healed, I had been pain free for weeks, and I was even fitting back into my pre pregnancy clothes (though the belly was here to stay!)

At 5 weeks old I took littlest man to baby clinic to get weighed (I'm going to gloss over the fact that I actually took him the day before too.... that I managed in the fog of my baby brain to go to the right place at the right time.... just on the wrong day and made a fool of myself hammering on the door and pressing the buzzer until someone actually answered and explained that I was there a day early!)

Anyway, my stupidity aside, not only had he gained weight, he had actually jumped up a centile on his growth chart! The health visitor actually congratulated me on doing a brilliant job of feeding him and I came away feeling so glad that we had his tongue tie cut, and incredibly happy that I persevered and stood my ground to exclusively breast fed....it would've been so easy to give up, but I was SO proud that we didn't.

Of course, in true style he decided to celebrate this great achievement by wanting to feed approximately every half an hour from 2.30am that night just to remind me how good we were at it! Still, sleep is for the weak anyway right?!

I honestly never thought we would make it that far.

Before he was born, I was setting myself goals of doing it for the first few days, then for 2 weeks until hubby went back to work, but now it just seemed so easy, so natural (and that's before I even began to think about how much time we were saving not sterilising and making bottles – I clearly remembered how exhausting I found that last time round.... and how much money we were saving not buying formula!)

Realising that week that I had started to watch daytime tv made me determined that we were going to start getting out of the house more, as lovely as it was spending all of our days cuddled up and feeding, I was beginning to need some adult conversation and finally felt ready to show off my smallest boy to the world.

I had a few comments over the first few weeks about the fact that our newest addition was the absolute image of his big sister. In fact, within a few minutes of him being born all I could see was her, he had the exact same colour and amount of hair – completely different to my other 2 boys – the same colouring and the same little nose and chubby cheeks.

The first thing my mum said when she saw him was that he was the image of her too. I have to admit it took me by surprise, and knocked me sideways slightly, but I now LOVED the fact he looked so much like his big sister.

Another thing I had had to contend with recently was being asked many times – as I was many hundreds of times whilst I was pregnant – did I not want a girl?

Most of the people who asked that question are people who didn't know my past, so I guess I should forgive them?

127

But still…. REALLY?!

I don't understand why anybody would ask such a question out loud? To a new mother and a newborn baby? What even goes through people's minds? Do they have no filter between brain and mouth?!

I was over the moon with our new little man, and ecstatic that we had another little boy in our lives. I'd have loved a little girl, exactly the same as I love our little boy. No more and no less.

In all honesty upon knowing we had a little boy I was relieved that I wouldn't be seeing all of those "firsts" that I missed with her with another little girl. I'm not sure how I'd have coped with a baby girl, and as littlest man looked so like his big sister, I think a little girl looking like her might've been much harder to deal with. I don't know though, and in all honesty its irrelevant.

So yes, I was happy that I had 3 boys, even happier that both boys got the little brother they wished for.

Alongside all of this was the laughter and eye rolling at the amount of "breastfeeding" their dolls my nieces had been doing lately, whenever we were together, I could often be found sat feeding little man with a row of 2/3/4 little girls sat alongside me with dolls up their jumpers, it was amazing!

My 5-year-old niece also decided it was her time to ask lots of questions about baby loss. In fact, I'm pretty sure her exact words were:

"You've had 2 babies that died in your belly…. ewwww yuk!! And (my daughter) ….so you've had 3 babies that died?"

There was also "Did you kill her?"

And "Did a bad man shoot you in the belly and kill her?"

Many people might cringe at the thought of all these questions and wonder how on earth I could deal with them, but in all honesty, I am glad she asked them, and even more glad that I was at a point where I could answer them honestly and laugh about it.

I was glad that in a world where there's so much stigma attached to baby loss, a world where people just don't want to talk about it, that that 5-year-old little girl could speak so openly about it, that she could ask questions, that she could want to understand…. in fact, I'm proud that all of the children in my family know so much about it, because I hope that in time, they will grow into adults that aren't afraid to talk about it either. That should there be a time in their lives where someone they know or love experiences anything similar (I seriously hope not) that they will not shy away from them, that they will be able to speak about loss as openly as they do now.

My main hope was that all of these little people would grow into compassionate big people, because that would mean that I wouldn't be fighting the battle to break the taboo on my own, I had this whole army of small people normalising it with me.

So, yes, our family was finally complete, and yes, I was incredibly blessed and really was happier than I had been in such a long time, but below the surface there was still SO much going on, my past experiences were not something that would ever go away.

Baby loss was a part of me, it had made me who I am and even though grief was not at the forefront of my mind anymore, although I really was happy and contented and enjoying life, that didn't mean I was healed or that I had forgotten…. My daughter had still died; I had still had 2 miscarriages.

I had been pregnant 6 times to get to this point and I could never forget any of them, nor did I want to.

TWENTY SEVEN

One morning when smallest boy was a couple of months old, I attended a meeting of my local LLL group, the subject being "breastfeeding and body image" …. my first thoughts on the subject when I saw the topic were that it was not something I'd thought too much about, but the more I thought about it since the more I realised that that really wasn't the case.

I didn't have the confidence to tell my whole story to the group, so I sat listening to the other women in the room discussing issues around body image and it stirred up a lot of thought.

Although I was now 100% confident breastfeeding smallest boy whenever and wherever we were, regardless of who may or may not be watching, it made me a little sad to say that this was only a very recent occurrence, and that body image – or body confidence – was a huge part of why I didn't breastfeed last time round.

I suppose I should start from the beginning.

I was only 19 years old when my daughter was born, and even if she had survived, I wouldn't have even attempted to breastfeed her.

I can honestly say the thought hadn't even crossed my mind throughout my pregnancy, in my head babies had bottles and that was that. We had bought bottles and formula very early on in my pregnancy and there wasn't really ever any mention that I would do anything else.

As things worked out, in her incredibly short life she had neither breast nor bottle.

11 months later when my biggest boy was born, my 20-year-old head was still firmly bottles and formula – I knew nothing else. My friends all used bottles, nothing else even crossed my mind.

This time though my baby was in neonatal intensive care and the nurses there told me that breastmilk was good for premature and sick babies and encouraged me to express for him. Of course, I did, I'd have done anything to keep my boy alive, but I'll openly admit that I HATED every single minute of it.

Sat attached to a pump every couple of hours day and night for a fortnight was not my idea of fun, I was home without my baby, and still up every 2 hours to express milk, then travelling for up to an hour at least twice a day with my cool bag to get it back to the hospital and to see my baby. I hated it.

I only got to actually breastfeed him twice, and that was with him covered in tubes and wires next to his incubator with a screen around us. I had no idea what I was doing and there was no support available. I didn't exactly enjoy the experience; it was all quite surreal.

Needless to say, when the Drs told me after 2 weeks that he couldn't have breast milk anymore, that he needed a specialised formula I wasn't sad…. just relieved that I didn't have to pump anymore.

My past experience, plus my lack of body confidence meant that once again 4 years later when having my next baby, aged 23, I still didn't contemplate breastfeeding. Although by then I saw it as a "normal" thing to do, I just didn't have the confidence in myself to do it, the thought of getting my boob out in front of anyone made me want to run for the hills!

So, I used bottles and formula and never thought twice about it.

A lot had changed since then though.

Back then I hated my body.

The stretch marks that covered my stomach from the polyhydramnios I had suffered from with my first 2 pregnancies, and from being pregnant with my huge 3rd baby... I hated them with a passion.

If someone had offered me surgery to remove them, I'd have taken it without question.

I hated the scars from my 3 Caesarean sections.

The wrinkled pouch of stomach that no matter what I did just wouldn't go away. I could barely even look at it.

I hated the way my body looked.

Fast forward a few years and now I hated my body even more.

Not only had it created 2 such seriously ill babies, but now it had put me and hubby though 3 years of unexplained infertility and subjected us to fertility drugs and the horror of 2 missed miscarriages and the 2 lots of surgery afterwards.

By the time I became pregnant for the 6th time aged 30 it's safe to say I didn't have a positive thought left about my body, there were times when I was so consumed in hatred for it, for it "not working properly" and for it looking so hideous.

My hubby would constantly tell me that I was wrong, that my body was beautiful, that it had given me my children, that I should be proud of it, but his words fell upon deaf ears, I didn't want to hear them.

As far as I was concerned my body was broken, and I hated it.

But now, for perhaps the first time in my life, I felt something other than loathing for my body.

I remember saying to my hubby "every time I look at our smallest little man, I am amazed that he has grown so much and that it's all down to me.... that my body is doing what it should be and feeding this little man everything he needs". I was as shocked as he was to hear those words coming out of my mouth.

But it was true. Breastfeeding had given me back confidence in my body. Both in the physical sense that I was happy to just get out a boob and feed him, and in that I was past caring about my body image, past caring what anyone else thought, when he was hungry all that mattered was that he was fed, it didn't even cross my mind to be self-conscious!

It had also proven to me that my body wasn't broken after all. It had carried a perfectly healthy little boy, and it was feeding him and helping him grow.

I felt a massive sense of achievement, like a weight had been lifted from me.

I was no longer wasting energy hating my body, I no longer cared what anyone else thought about me feeding my baby.

For the first time ever, my body was doing everything right, and although I still didn't like what I saw in the mirror (though I'm pretty sure nobody does post-partum) and although I knew that my stretch marks and scars were always going to be there hidden away, for the first time in 13 years, finally at the age of 31, I could honestly say that I was proud of my body and what it had achieved.

It had given me 4 beautiful children, and was exclusively feeding one of them, I had every reason to be proud of it.

Only a couple of days later I had my postnatal check. Everything was fine, I had my iron levels rechecked, got retested for group b strep, my Caesarean scar was all healed. But after looking at my scar etc the Dr decided to refer me to a physiotherapist because of the dire state of my stomach muscles.... this is where that fine line between laughter and tears comes in!

A few years earlier, I'd have cried even at the thought of the Dr seeing my stomach, that day I laughed.... laughed that after nearly 13 years she'd decided it needed fixing, laughed that I actually no longer cared what it looked like!

Physiotherapy might make a difference, but if it didn't.... who cares??!

My body had given me my 4 beautiful children.... I would sacrifice my stomach muscles a million times over for that!

TWENTY EIGHT

Half term was now in full swing, I had all 4 of our children and we were all still alive.... That was a victory in my eyes!

Seriously though, the biggest 3 spent all day playing so nicely together that it made my heart melt a little.... they all adored each other (at least some of the time) and to be honest I don't think we could've asked for much more than that.

I've always said I would be concerned if they were the best of friends all of the time (Though a little more often certainly wouldn't go amiss!!)

The next day though my biggest boy made me very proud, the day started with an appointment for him that he REALLY didn't like, the kind that generally meant tears beforehand and him being in a foul mood.

This day was no exception!

Trying to get out of the house with him that morning wasn't exactly fun for anybody... however, after all of that drama, middle boy (it still felt weird not calling him littlest boy!) was upset, and his big brother after realising this, then spent all afternoon doing anything and everything he could to cheer him up.

We went to the shop and he bought him some sweets, and even humoured him with a game of "building a den and turning it into a chocolate museum".

The pair of them were hidden underneath the dining table cuddled up and giggling away to themselves for the best part of 2 hours! It was moments like this that made all the shite parts of parenthood disappear, watching him comfort and entertain his little brother when there were probably a million things he'd rather be doing.

It's times like those that made me take a step back and see just how lucky I was. We had created our own little army of strong willed, crazy, loud, hard work, frustrating, exhausting little people.... and I'm not afraid to admit that half of the time their arguments, the constant bickering and fighting made me want to cry.... but then out of nowhere, one of these perfect little moments came along and made me so proud of them, because they might be far from perfect and some days, I would kill for a half an hour break...

BUT they were also fiercely protective of each other, loyal, loving and caring – we just didn't step back enough to see that every day in the craziness of daily life. We're usually too wrapped up in hectic day to day stuff to stop for long enough and notice the little things.... I was normally too busy shouting at them to get shoes on and brush their teeth, or frantically trying to cook their tea with littlest man attached to my boob whilst shouting through the house for them all to get changed and fill their drink bottles up so that we could all get out of the house for their taekwondo lesson in time!

We lived our lives too wrapped up in daily routines to pause for long enough to listen to them making plans for tomorrow, to listen to their laughter as they recalled something funny that they all did together earlier, to see the quick kiss they gave their little brother every time they walked past, to listen to them sneaking into each other's rooms for a cuddle before bed.

But then some days they did something that made me stop for long enough to realise that everything was fine, that they didn't all hate each other really, and that gave me hope that in years to come they would always have each other's backs.... That the bond between them was so strong and despite all the bickering they loved each other dearly... and when it matters the most the kind, caring little traits overcome the fighting... and we could all live happily ever after for at least a few hours.

TWENTY NINE

By the time he was 3 months old smallest boy had a diagnosis of eczema. After a few weeks of us trying to manage it with oils etc I finally gave in and took him to the GP who confirmed that it was definitely eczema and started him on some treatment. Initially he was to be bathed in paraffin and be completely covered from head to toe in cream 4 times a day.

Within only a couple of days he already seemed happier and more settled...so the ridiculous amount of time it seemed to be taking me to undress him, cover him in cream, and dress him again several times a day seemed to be worthwhile.

Sadly, this didn't last long. By the weekend it seemed he was having a reaction to his new cream, he was completely covered in a horrible rash and understandably very grumpy.

It made me sad, sad that he was suffering, and sad that there was barely anything I could do to fix it.... I'm not good when there's no magic cure!

I was tired.... tired of spending all of my time and energy overthinking what I could do for him, when every answer I could come up basically meant - not very much.

When your day has been so bad even chocolate won't fix it, you know it's been bad.

When it's only 6.30pm and you're wanting/needing to get into bed you know it's been bad.

When you can hear one child singing a song about how much he hates you in one room, and another child banging around, muttering to himself about things not being fair in another room, whilst the smallest child has spent the majority of the day crying you know it's been bad.

Just a small snapshot of my day, I ended up spending 10 minutes locked in the bathroom with a small child attached to my boob just for a bit of headspace...

Motherhood wasn't always fun.

But I kept reminding myself, even in the hardest moments, it was all worth it.

Hubby said something over the weekend that put it all into perspective though. He said that he was sad that he'd got eczema as it was obviously hereditary from him.... when I thought of the hereditary condition, he could've got from me (and didn't) I found some fighting spirit, I reckoned we could deal with a bit of eczema no problem!

THIRTY

On International Women's Day, when smallest boy was almost 4 months old, I read a LOT of posts online about inspirational women.

I was spending my afternoon underneath a grumpy, itchy sleepy baby, so had a lot of time to think about the women who had influenced me and my life.

I am incredibly lucky to have spent my early life and childhood surrounded by amazing women, my mum and my nan being the 2 strongest, most amazing women I have ever met. I lived with them both from being only young, these 2 incredible women brought up me and my sister, through some really tough (and also really amazing) times.

As we got older, after my parents split up there were a few years where we referred to ourselves as "the 4 musketeers" we were a force to be reckoned with!

Sadly, a few years earlier we slowly started losing my nan to Alzheimer's, and we mourned the loss of her as the woman she once was way before she lost her battle with life. But even right up until the end, we saw glimpses of her strong character, she really was the kindest, most generous person you could ever meet.

Throughout Nans battle with Alzheimer's were several truly awful experiences, both with hospital admissions and care homes, which only made the remaining "3 musketeers" stronger.... we had battles to fight for our Nan, we had to get her the care she so deserved, and we didn't stop until she was being well looked after and happy.... it took a lot of hard work and determination, but we eventually did.... even with just the 3 of us, we could face any battle, fight any fight that we needed to.

I owe all of my strength and resilience to these amazing women.

Now, in my adult life, alongside my mum and my sister, I had several fantastic, strong, amazing women who I am lucky enough to call my friends (you know who you are!) and had also recently joined a couple of groups full of amazing women.... I felt so incredibly lucky to be surrounded by and supported by so many incredible women.... together we could achieve anything.

Healing is a term I haven't used very often in regard to my experience of baby loss, or anything else to be fair, but it seems like the only word to use right now.

Just days after international women's day came Mother's Day, a day I usually dreaded, though not a day I could ignore as my own Mum is amazing and she deserved a little recognition at least.

For the first time ever, Mother's Day was actually a really lovely day. Yes, I visited the cemetery, and yes, I shed a couple of tears, but after that I had a really lovely day spending time with my little family... all 4 of our living children and my hubby, and later on with our bigger family too.

There were no long lie ins, presents or flowers (other than some I bought myself) because none of that is needed in our house, I really meant it when I said my children are all I need... just some lovely cards and some chocolates they had all spent hours making together for me, and a lovely day spent all together, having fun and making memories – I really couldn't have asked for anything more.

I'd had brief conversations with a couple of friends in the past couple of months about healing…. and I honestly felt like the arrival of our smallest boy had helped me to heal in so many ways.

Of course, I would never "get over" losing my darling girl, and I would never forget our experiences of infertility and miscarriage, but I felt like our family was complete now, and although my daughter would always be the missing piece, there would always be that hole where she should be, that grief was just not so raw these days.

I had many fights with my conscious over this time and time again, but I had come to realise that I was strong enough now to know that however I felt, however I grieved, it was all completely normal and individual…. moving on with life is not the same as forgetting… crying fewer tears didn't mean my love had faded any.

For probably the first time in 12 years I didn't spend the majority of Mother's Day feeling sad and miserable… I smiled, and it wasn't forced.

I allowed myself to have fun and not feel guilty about it. Grief was no longer at the forefront of my mind, and I had learnt that that was ok. Grief changes…. it doesn't disappear, it just evolves.

It meant that I no longer felt guilty for being happy. Life was busy, hard work and exhausting at times, but so rewarding and full of happiness too.

We may have been exhausted and completely skint… but we couldn't wish for anymore love…. love is what heals, it's what gets us through the toughest times, and what makes the best times even better.

Love is what made Mother's Day bearable, enjoyable even. And I was finally ok with that. It seemed like a massive moment for me, allowing myself to feel happiness override my grief and pain.

A few weeks later, my morning started grumpily. Littlest man was up at least 6 times in the night (instead of his usual 2 – yes, I know I was lucky he slept so well normally!) so I was exhausted.

I was then reminded by middle boy how long it was until our holidays which made me panic about saving up (or lack of) etc, so it's safe to say by the time I'd done the school run and spent 2 hours cleaning whilst rocking a grumpy baby I was pretty fed up.

I sat down for 5 minutes peace and saw a few things posted online telling me that it was "international happiness day". So instead of using my few minutes peace to sit and eat biscuits and feel sorry for myself I decided to pull myself together, stop being grumpy and focus on the things in my life that made me happy.

Firstly had to be my children of course – they were the reason I got up every day, the reason I lived and breathed, the reason I smiled even when I didn't feel like smiling (in fact ESPECIALLY when I didn't feel like smiling) they were my life, my world, and even when they drove me absolutely round the bend and pushed my patience to the limit (which to be completely honest was most days!!) they had all brought immense happiness to my life and continued to do so every single day.

Of course I'd be lying if I said they made me happy all of the time, there were days/times when they could reduce me to tears (the biggest boys at least – though I was sure in time smallest boy would develop the ability to do that too) but that's what being a mum is all about isn't it? Taking the rough with the smooth, being that person, they can take all their frustration and anger out on safely, and the happiness far outweighed anything else.

Watching them together is what made me the happiest, watching the love the bigger ones had for their baby brother was amazing and made all the difficult moments fade into the distance, and seeing smallest boys face light up when he saw them after they've spent all day at school was priceless.

My long-suffering husband should probably come next, although he drives me almost as mad as the kids do some days there's no one I'd rather have by my side on this incredible journey (I could go on and on about how amazing he is - in fact, that could be a whole chapter in itself – but if he happens to read this id never hear the end of it so I'll keep it short!)

He works A LOT to provide for us all, so that I can stay home with the kids and for that I'll be forever grateful. He makes sacrifices for us all, all of the time, and he is the most amazing daddy to our 2 smallest boys (and my stepdaughter) and a brilliant stepdad to biggest boy too.

He had been my rock for the past 7 1/2 years and brought so much happiness into my life…. our little family may be put together differently than most but it's bloody amazing and is the main source of happiness in my life.

His love and support had such a huge impact on my parenting choices this time round, and on my confidence, something for which I would be forever grateful.

My incredible family have to come next – I talk a lot about my "little family" and my "bigger family", I am lucky to be so close to them and equally our children are so lucky to be growing up with so many close family members.

I am told frequently by many people how lucky I am to have my parents so close by and how lucky our children are being surrounded by grandparents etc.... I have to admit that to me that's just normal.... I grew up a few doors down from my grandparents, and after my grandad died when I was only young my nan came and lived with us, I was so incredibly close to her, and I am so grateful that our children have the opportunity to be so close to their extended family too.

We are blessed with 6 beautiful nieces too, 6 cousins for our children to grow up alongside, each of them bringing even more happiness (and often chaos!) into our lives.

Alongside a handful of close friends who I love dearly and have been there throughout the good and the bad, I really couldn't ask for much more.

My morning stress seemed insignificant now – I realised that we were lucky to be going on holiday – the opportunity to spend a whole week together as a family having fun and making even more memories – memories that the kids (and us grown-ups) will laugh and smile about for many years – money seemed pretty insignificant in all that.

I realised that day that I had a lot in my life to be happy about. Those things that made me unhappy and grumpy were pretty insignificant and sometimes (far too often) I wasted too much time and energy stressing about the little things... things that were either insignificant or that I had no control over.

I made it my mission to not stress the little things in life.

THIRTY ONE

By this time, our smallest boy was no longer a "newborn" and was changing so incredibly quickly, he had developed his own little personality, a gorgeous smile and the most beautiful laugh.... in a way I missed the newborn stage already but knowing that we were never going to do this again made me cherish every single moment.

Every new day and new change in him made me so incredibly happy and proud too.... watching him giggling and playing with his toys melted my heart every single time. I still on occasion couldn't quite believe he was really here and that he was really ours!

That week had brought with it more giggles, and a new round of eczema treatment – which seemed to be working a lot better than the previous ones. We were now on a regime of 3 different creams, a total of 8 times a day – at 6 separate times.... It seemed pretty full on and very time consuming – but we were hopeful it would be worth it and get it under control.

A reflux diagnosis and new medications to try had been another plus, they seemed to begin working and I was desperate for them to mean we could get some more sleep.

I had never heard of the 4 month sleep regression until this point – and we were certainly living through it.

I was exhausted. It was almost the Easter holidays, and we were all looking forward to some much-needed family time (and hoping for a little sunshine too – or at least no more snow... I needed spring to arrive!)

It seemed like such a distant memory, but last Easter weekend had been when we found out our smallest little man was on his way.

It felt like YEARS ago to be honest, though I think his pregnancy made for 9 of the longest months of my life so far.

Last Easter had been quite different to this one, we were happy of course – we'd given up the hope that we'd ever have another baby by then after over 4 years of trying, but we were also terrified – after 2 heart-breaking missed miscarriages the previous year we had almost no strength, and zero hope left.... I don't think any of us even dared to imagine that we'd be spending this Easter with our family complete.

The school holidays were ending with smallest man's christening, exactly a year after we found out I was pregnant, what better date to celebrate how lucky we were to have him.

I am not a religious person at all, my children went to a church school but that's because it was our local school not because of religion.

I didn't go to church unless it was for a special occasion, or for something the kids were doing through school, although I do have to admit that I did love that they were part of a church school, I loved their sense of belonging to the church and I loved going to church to watch their services etc.

It's not that I was anti religion at all – in fact, I was sometimes a little envious of people who have strong beliefs, but for me, religion had just never really played a big part in my life.

It's not something I spent much time even considering – maybe that's wrong of me?! But in all honesty, I probably lost what little faith I might have had when I was younger after losing my beautiful girl.

We chose not to get married in church because we didn't believe it was the right thing to do as we don't actively practice religion. None of our other children have been christened – we had naming ceremonies for both big boys which were held in a church and led by a vicar, but they weren't actually christened because we chose not to, we felt it would be a little hypocritical of us to christen our children into a faith we don't actively practice.

So, it may seem a little ridiculous after reading all this that we chose to have our beautiful boy christened at all!

BUT there was a reason of course, whatever I may or may not believe, several people close to us spent a lot of time and energy praying that we would get to bring home a happy healthy baby, and of course we did.

Even my completely non-religious hubby decided that finding out that I was pregnant on Easter Sunday and being due on Christmas Day was some kind of sign that everything would be ok this time…. he took some small degree of comfort in that, and it helped him to believe that things would be ok, he took the decision upon himself to ask people we knew to include us in their prayers, and he made a promise to himself that should we get to bring a healthy baby home with us, that he would take them to church.

Who knows whether prayers were answered?

Who knows whether it was some kind of sign?

Who am I to make that decision?

BUT .... he was here, safe and well, and lots of people took the time to pray for him, and for us, and whether the outcome has anything to do with them or not we will never truly know.

So, all we could do was be grateful, grateful that they cared enough to try, grateful that they felt they could use their faith to help us, and above all else, grateful to have our beautiful boy with us.

The decision to have him christened was not taken lightly, but we felt a massive need to say thank you, to celebrate our beautiful boy with all of those people who had been alongside us throughout our very long journey.

We decided that getting him christened could only be a good thing, and that although we didn't regularly take him to church, and I didn't anticipate that changing, we had decided that people's prayers for him could never be a bad thing.

We chose godparents for him carefully, and after a lot of thought and consideration we chose 6 people who we knew loved him dearly and who we wanted to be a part of his life forever on journey through life, just as they had helped us on our journey to get him here.

We all had a lovely day, the 3 biggest kids took part in the service in some way, it was personal, and at points filled with laughter as well as thanksgiving.

We were surrounded by so many family and friends, and we celebrated afterwards with lots of cake and catching up with people we just didn't see often enough.

Our beautiful boy was surrounded by all of the people who love him, and was spoilt with love, cards and gifts, we felt incredibly lucky.

THIRTY TWO

The next few weeks were pretty hectic, smallest boy had been poorly, there were several GP trips, an out of hours trip, several new medications with varying results.

On top of that, hubby was recovering from a vasectomy which he required endless sympathy for yet got none!

Smallest boys' latest diagnosis was hay fever/allergies and possibly (allergic) asthma too. So, antihistamines (that had to be prescribed unlicensed as there was nothing licensed for his age... that then made him WAY too sleepy) and inhalers alongside his new sunglasses (to keep the pollen out- though they had earnt us some funny looks!) Vaseline (to smear around his nose and mouth to try and do the same) and nose drops were now sitting alongside his Gaviscon and eczema creams in a seemingly never-ending cycle of trying to keep him happy.

It had been one hell of a week to say the least.

It did get me thinking though.

Even though the past couple of weeks had been hard work with smallest man, things were SO incredibly different and so much easier than they had been at this stage with any of my other children.

5 months after having my beautiful girl I was still in the darkest place of grief (and also in the early stages of pregnancy).

5 months after having biggest boy we were in a weird kind of new normal, with daily visits from nurses, at least weekly hospital visits, and a mass of medications, tubes and monitors.

When middle boy was 5 months old, I was living alone with 2 small boys, me and hubby had just got together, and I was in the middle of a court battle.

All 3 times, my heart was full of love, but life was far from easy.

Fast forward to now, when smallest boy was 5 months old and looking back certainly put things into perspective.... yes, there had been struggles and worries, but life was amazing.

This week was my baby girl's birthday, and that was always going to be tough as I thought of all that should have been and relived all the memories I had safely stored away.

But I had my wonderful hubby by my side, my 3 boys to hold onto, and the knowledge that life was so much happier and easier now than it has been for a very long time.

I just needed to ride out the storm, let myself grieve once more and hold my boys close. I knew I would never stop missing my beautiful baby girl, there will NEVER be a way to find a positive in losing her, but I would always be thankful that I am her mummy, and grateful for all that having her had taught me.

Life was very different to how it had ever been.

Different in a good way. Our crazy, dysfunctional, unorthodox, untraditional family was happy and complete, and with them and the rest of our family and friends by my side, even the shittiest of weeks could still contain smiles and laughter.

As her birthday came and went it felt rather strange (and perhaps I felt a little guilty) to admit that this year I seemed to have coped far better than I ever had before.

I know my baby loss friends will be with me in saying that it's usually the few days before and after that are the hardest, and I'm not ashamed to admit that usually I would spend each day for a few days before up until 8 days after (the day of her funeral) reliving exactly what happened at each moment all those years ago.

From my last scan and amnio drainage on the morning of her birth, to every single visitor. From the last time I held her, to going to visit her in the chapel of rest, and then to her funeral.

This year, although all of those things were in the back of my mind each day, that's all they were.

Of course, I was sad, and I shed tears for my beautiful girl on her birthday, and all that should've been, but I carried on as normal, I didn't lock myself away from the world, in fact I spent the day of her birthday surrounded by my closest friends - all 4 of smallest boys' godmothers, and for the first time ever I laughed and smiled all day long.... I was absolutely exhausted by the end of the day, and very full of biscuits.... but relieved that I had made it through in one piece.

For the next week I was on holiday with all of my family (as we always were this week of every year – so that's not what made it different) and since we got back, I had spent 3 lovely days with my little family.

I wasn't sure how I should feel, happy that I had coped so well, or guilty that maybe that meant I had moved on?

I knew I'd never get over losing my precious girl, and I'd never stop loving her or missing her, but I realised I should be thankful that life was so good at the moment that I could still smile even on the bad days.

Maybe that whole cliche of time being a healer is somewhat true... or maybe I was just lucky and next year it would be horrendous again?

Who knows?

I realised that even this far along the journey it was still unpredictable, and I just had to ride out whatever feelings and emotions I came across.

I had learnt to cherish the good days and ride out the bad ones.

THIRTY THREE

Our smallest boy was 6 months old. It was hard to recall or even imagine the sheer terror I had been feeling 6 months earlier as I anxiously awaited his birth.

The past 6 months had brought immeasurable joy, happiness, a little tiredness (not enough to complain about generally) and a few stresses, but 99.9% euphoria and a general feeling of completeness.

I was well aware that I was turning into one of those annoying mother's posting a million pictures of my beautiful baby using terrible cliches like #soblessed etc and I really didn't care!

I had a very select group of people on my social media accounts for the very reason that I didn't need or want the whole world to see my children.

Anyway, I digress....

The past week had brought a new reflux medication (that we were yet to see any benefits from) and the introduction of food which had been fun! It had also seen him well and truly on the move, he could get from one side of the room to the other quicker than I could turn round, there was no stopping him!

Baby led weaning was a whole new journey for me as well as for him, and it was testing the limits of my mess handling skills! It was going to be a long slow process, especially for a boy who loved nothing more than boob.... But it seemed to be going ok so far.

After a particularly "challenging" evening with middle boy a few days later, followed by a not so brilliant morning, I was feeling particularly exhausted. I sat down to eat some lunch and was contemplating doing some kind of housework whilst smallest boy slept, but instead I (rather guiltily) chose to let him fall asleep on me and sat and read a book a lovely friend had lent me.

It was the first time I had just sat and done "nothing" in a couple of weeks, life had been ridiculously busy just lately, but I still felt guilty for taking half an hour to just sit and cuddle him whilst he slept when there were so many jobs that needed doing.

The books title "what mother's do especially when it looks like nothing" said it all really, I was quite often found saying that I had "done nothing all day" when I guess the reality was far from that.

I had also recently found myself feeling guilty when conversations had come up about when I would be going back to work and my reply had been that I wasnt anytime soon...

It seemed ridiculous really, I was not ashamed of my choice to be a stay-at-home mum, because it was exactly that ... a choice... a choice made by me and hubby that we were both happy with, and that worked for our little family.

We had to make sacrifices so that it was financially doable, but we knew that before we even thought about extending our family, and it was a decision we made together, about the right thing for us all.

So yes, we had to be extremely careful with money and cut back on extravagant things like gifts, days/nights out and holidays, but that's a choice we had happily made.

Acceptance was a massive thing for me, something which I thought a lot about.

Over the past few months, I had been trying incredibly hard to learn to accept things that were out of my control, not to dwell on things that I couldn't change, and not to let the behaviours or attitudes of others affect me.

Initially I was trying to do all this for myself, to let me enjoy life more with less stress and drama, to give space to and to protect my newfound happiness and confidence, so that I could be a happier, better mum to our little tribe.

More recently though I had found myself using the term "acceptance" more and more for our children's sake.

Not only in accepting people's differences – they were already very good at accepting many things such as disability or sexuality, but we had been working hard in encouraging them to accept other people's wishes and feelings, even if they didn't understand them, or agree with them.

Helping them to accept that other people's actions were sometimes hard to understand, trying to make them realise that challenging other people or questioning their feelings or actions wasn't always the answer. Letting them realise that however hard it may be, sometimes just accepting and moving on was the only way.

Teaching the art of acceptance to them was important, of course so that they could learn to accept other people's differences, but it is also a useful tool for them to use at any time of life.

Whenever they saw, heard or read something that made them question themselves or others, whenever they felt hard done to as a consequence of other people's actions or simply when they were tired of making excuses for other people's behaviour.

After doing all that we could, all we had left to do was hope.

Hope that one day they would pass on the concept of acceptance to others, and that maybe one day the rest of the world would learn to be as accepting as they were.

Deep down I couldn't have cared less about anyone else's opinion.... but that didn't stop the tiny guilty feeling every time I said it out loud, didn't stop the need for me to explain and justify our decisions.

I was loving every minute of motherhood this time round and was so much more confident than I ever had been before, not only in my parenting choices, but also in myself, which was lucky given smallest boys' mission to have me whip out a boob everywhere I went! A year earlier, I couldn't even imagine myself feeding in public... oh how far we had come!

The introduction of food and the fact that he was now over 6 months old had prompted several comments recently.

Comments that I should be breastfeeding him less, or on the fact that he still fed several times in the night, or even asking when I was going to stop.

In all honesty before I started this journey, I had never imagined we'd make it this far, to get past the official guidelines to exclusively breastfeed up until 6 months felt like a massive achievement and now, I didn't know when we would stop.

I hadn't set myself a new goal. The WHO guidelines to feed up until 2 years old seemed like a million miles away but we had decided to just take one day at a time and see what happened.

What I did know was that right now it worked for us, and I was so proud of how far we had come.

Reading the book made me realise that I was never "doing nothing".

Just in the past hour and a half I had:

Ordered the weekly food shop. Sorted out some bills that needed paying. Written lists. Checked emails. Replied to a couple of texts. Mentally sorted tea for us all...

All whilst feeding my baby.

My extremely happy, smiley little boy who had more than doubled in size in the past 6 months.... and I was the only person who could take any credit for that. (I can 99% accurately say that the minuscule amounts of food he had consumed over the past 2/3 weeks hadn't had that much of an effect!)

So, if nurturing this little man was "all" I achieved some days whilst the others were at school then so what?!

The ironing could wait. Time passes by too quickly, all too soon he wouldn't want to fall asleep on my chest, or feed to sleep. Someday soon enough he would be as independent as his big brothers and I would miss these days of doing "nothing".

I would never regret holding my baby for too long.

THIRTY FOUR

All of our children liked to cause a little bit of drama now and again, just to keep us on our toes and make sure we didn't get too complacent.

At 7 months old it was smallest boys turn and he did it in magnificent style, with impeccable timing…

We had been incredibly careful whilst introducing foods to him doing it very slowly and one thing at a time over a few days so that we could see if anything triggered his eczema, and despite a couple of really small flare ups after eating certain vegetables everything had been fine, in fact his eczema had improved dramatically over previous weeks.

So, one evening whilst the big boys were having omelette for their tea, I cut a small piece off for smallest boy to try.

He played with it for a few minutes, nibbled the corner from it then dropped it down underneath his high chair tray. I tried to put my hand down to give it back to him and couldn't reach, so took off the tray to get it out. As I removed the tray, I noticed his stomach was bright red and covered in a rash, I picked up the omelette and as I looked up at him realised his mouth and face were also breaking out in the same rash.

I quickly undid the high chair to take him out, ringing my sister and my mum on speaker as I did it to try and get someone to come sit with the bigger boys so that I could go to the drs… before I'd got off the phone I realised his face was starting to swell up, and quickly ran out of the front door with him whilst on the phone to the GP telling them I was on my way –

luckily we lived a 2 minute walk from our GP and as we arrived they were at the door waiting for us.

By the time we got into the surgery and undressed him, less than 5 minutes from leaving home, my poor baby had huge handprints of the rash under his armpits and on his back where I had been carrying him after touching the omelette.

Luckily, he was given medicine and within 2-3 minutes it had started to come down.... which is more than I can say for my stress levels by that point!

Within a few days, and after a lot of research into egg allergies, I had realised that the "insect bites" we had thought he'd had many times over the past few months hadn't been bites after all but contact reactions.

We spent a lot of time telling the bigger boys over and over again about the importance of hand washing after touching food. Within the first week or so after diagnosis we realised he was having small reactions after people had touched him or kissed him after eating foods containing eggs... spots we'd previously put down to either eczema or bites, but now of course we knew better.

We felt so lucky. Lucky, that it happened at home, 2 minutes away from the (open) doctor's surgery, and lucky that I realised what was happening before he ate any. Lucky that we had family 2 minutes away who could come round in an instant and watch the bigger boys (typically it happened the only night that hubby had gone out straight from work and so wasn't home at teatime) and most of all lucky that smallest boy was completely oblivious to all the drama that occurred and was now absolutely fine.

The summer holidays passed in a whirlwind of sunshine and fun. Smallest boy learnt to crawl and loved exploring the grass and being outside with his brothers and sister. We had a lovely family holiday and were all really enjoying life.

We were all sad when the holidays were over, and normality resumed.

In September, just after they big ones had gone back to school, I left my smallest boy for the very first time (for longer than an hour at least). It was my sisters 30th birthday and we went out for a day of spa treatments, food and cocktails.

To say I was stressed about leaving him would be a bit of an understatement! He was very much a boob monster – refusing bottles and cups of any description, and he had spent 2 weeks refusing to eat food due to the appearance of his first tooth.

However, I went out and left him for 11 hours, and whilst I was gone, he ate 2 full meals and drank a bottle of expressed milk for daddy! In fact, I came home to him fast asleep in his cot with a very proud daddy and big brother – they'd all had a lovely day together!

I even had my first taste of alcohol in 2 and a half years! We worked out it had been that long since I last had a drink due to being pregnant on and off for 18 months before our smallest boy arrived and then breastfeeding ever since…I think it's safe to say I was even more of a lightweight than I used to be and after only 1 cocktail I needed to eat and have a lemonade!

We had a great day out celebrating though, and even managed a laugh whilst I was stood in the toilets with a pump down my dress expressing milk with an intrigued hen party!

As September passed us by, I was on a bit of a mission to get out a bit more with smallest boy and get to some toddler groups etc now he was on the move and actually wanting to play.

I had just taken him for his 9 month development check at our local clinic, having not had particularly good experiences at these kind of appointments with my bigger boys I wasn't really looking forward to it – my overriding memory of one with middle boy was them telling me off because he was still having a bottle in the night…. meaning that the next time I went I lied and told them what they wanted to hear so that I wasn't told off or judged.

I'd chatted with hubby and a couple of friends before I'd gone this time and said that I had every intention of telling them the truth this time, that I would be telling them that yes, he was still breastfed several times in the night, and yes, he did get in bed with us sometimes, and no I didn't actually care what they said he should or shouldn't be doing…. that we were doing what was best for us. I was very grateful for my increased confidence this time around!!

I was however pleasantly surprised, first of all I was actually congratulated for still breastfeeding, and when I politely declined her "night weaning" advice and said that in fact we were happy with what we were doing she said "I can't criticise if it works for you and your family" I was actually stunned!

In her words he was "following his growth curve like a breastfed baby does – perfectly" and earlier concerns about his soft spot were now gone. He was to be reassessed in a few months due to him "not meeting the fine motor skills target" and was referred to the hospital to have his eyes checked out but I wasn't at all concerned by any of those things.

She did tell me that he was doing well at following instructions which made me laugh a lot... I must have said "no don't climb on the fireplace" and moved him away 20 times that morning.... each time my "instruction" was met by laughter and him going straight back!

I reckoned he was a pretty "normal" 9 month old to be honest, he was doing just fine, I didn't need any professional or any check to tell me that I had a very happy healthy boy.

THIRTY FIVE

October soon came around and with it came baby loss awareness week. Social media was full of articles, quotes and photos from people like me who were trying to do their little bit to raise awareness and help other people.

Obviously, this was great, if it made people talk, made people question how they might react if someone they know or loved was to experience pregnancy or infant loss, then that was amazing.

All the media attention it seemed to have received meant that my newsfeed was even more full than previous years of other people's personal stories, these people (mainly although not all, women) had bared their hearts, their thoughts publicly, some had shared photos of their precious babies, all of which I imagine was tough for them (I know that personally despite sharing my thoughts often very publicly, I share photos of my daughter very rarely as I am wary of other people's reactions).

I have to say the support I saw these people get was amazing, with thousands of positive comments and shares, however, as always seems to be the case on social media, some of the comments I saw were just horrific.

I have in the past 16 years been on the receiving end of LOTS of stupid, mainly thoughtless comments, as have many people I know, and as much as I do tend to believe that they are mainly well intentioned, the more I read on social media the more I am seeing of them so I thought I'd share a few of my "favourites" in the hope that anybody who might read this would think twice

169

before using them in the future (in other words I thought I'd jump back up onto my soapbox and rant – humour me please!)

In no particular order are some of the things I have had said to me or I have seen said to others. (I should add that not all of these were in relation to baby loss, some were in relation to infertility, and miscarriage too).

The biggest one of all has to be, AT LEAST....

Please, please don't EVER start a sentence to somebody who has experienced pregnancy or infant loss, or infertility with these 2 words. It can never go well...

- At least she didn't live for weeks in hospital and then die... (why?? I'd have given anything to have spent more time with her while she was alive actually....)
- At least you're young, you can have another baby.... (like another baby will replace the daughter I have just buried?!)
- At least you have other children already.... (after a miscarriage) .... oh yes because that makes the loss of this pregnancy irrelevant, doesn't it?!
- At least it wasn't later in pregnancy... (34 weeks – practically full term....) what difference would it make being any later?! Or any earlier in fact??
- At least you didn't actually have to go through labour - I had a Caesarean to give her the best chance of survival- not exactly fun!
- At least you know you can get pregnant now (after the 2nd miscarriage in 6 months after 4 years of infertility) .... oh yes, because I only ever wanted to "get pregnant" - staying pregnant was not important at all...

- At least you can have fun trying again – trust me there is nothing "fun" about trying to conceive and failing miserably for 4 whole years.
- At least you've got each other – whilst somewhat true, I was very grateful for my supportive hubby and family but none of that takes away the grief unfortunately.

I'm sure there are "at least" another hundred of these that I've forgotten but you get the picture!

The next most common theme seems to be, it wasn't meant to be…God wanted her for himself…She was too special for this earth…now just isn't your time…

Regardless of your beliefs none of these comments are helpful to somebody who is in the early stages of grief and raw.

By all means pray for them if that's your thing, let them know you're praying for them or thinking of them – this will be appreciated so much more.

One of my personal favourites was said by my GP when I went to him to tell him I was pregnant again 3 months after my daughter died – I was incredibly anxious and also still struggling immensely with grief – his response – well what did you go and get pregnant again for if you're anxious?!…. very helpful thanks doctor!

Comparing grief is another massive no – no one person's grief is more important than another's – it's not a game of "I suffered more than you" every person's story, every person's journey is unique…. so please don't compare.

Miscarriage, stillbirth, neonatal death, the loss of a child at any age – all of these are traumatic, all different, yet all the same –

they are all the loss of a child, and no one has the right to tell anyone how they should feel.

I am happy to talk about my different experiences with neonatal death and miscarriage - having suffered both I am in a place where I can compare - in fact, the experiences of miscarriage for me were incredibly different each time.

But that is my personal experience, it is likely to be very different to anybody else's. It was personal and unique to me, to my family, to my situation, no two experiences however similar are ever going to evoke the exact same response or the exact same feelings.

It is not ok to say to any grieving parent - it could've been worse - it is not ok to undermine their grief or compare their grief to somebody else's in any way.

Time - it is absolutely not ok to imply that somebody should have "got over" their grief. Why is it ok for a person to mourn the loss of an adult friend or relative over long periods of time - to recognise important events, to miss them on special occasions, to honour them on birthdays and anniversaries, why if all this is "normal" is it not ok to do the same for our babies?!

Are you not over it yet it's been xxxx months/years?

Why anybody would even dream of asking this question is just beyond me to be honest!

One particular quote has always helped me - though I still haven't been brave enough to say it out loud but just thinking it in my head has helped... when somebody makes any of these comments, just take a deep breath and ask them - ok... so which of your children could you live without??

THIRTY SIX

I had never been under any illusion that parenting was supposed to be easy…. but I'm sure as mothers we have some kind of inbuilt filter that blocks out all the memories of the hard bits to ensure we forget before deciding we want to do it all over again!!

When smallest boy was 11 months old, we had a particularly tough few week. A teething (almost) toddler and an (almost) teenager had me wanting to tear my hair out…. who on earth decided having both of these particular breeds at same time was a good idea?! Oh yea, that would be me!

Of course, I have to say I loved them dearly, and I really wouldn't change anything at all, but those couple of weeks had been rough. I was surviving on very little sleep, was being constantly gnawed on by a little person I had nicknamed jaws (affectionately of course) …. who was not only very sad and grumpy thanks to the appearance of more teeth, but was also full of snot and had decided he wouldn't be put down for even 5 seconds most of the day, and on the very odd occasion he would it was only to practice his climbing skills on whatever piece of furniture was closest to him so involved me chasing after him and removing him over and over again whilst he laughed hysterically at me…?

It's probably no wonder that I had had a constant headache really!

All of that fun coupled with the teenage attitude/hormones/general 12-year-old boy stuff had meant that I spent far too much time either angry, arguing or in tears.... It hadn't been fun for anyone by any stretch of the imagination!

We had recently begun to realise that parenting with such a big age gaps although amazing in many ways, could be tough too.

The bond between the big boys and their little brother was amazing, it melted my heart every time I saw one of them playing with him and watching them pick out things they wanted to buy him for his birthday and Christmas and seeing how excited they were about him opening presents etc was lovely – they had written Christmas lists by this point and had chosen 20 times more things for him than they had for themselves!

But at the same time, pleasing them all at the same time was sometimes impossible, for example, deciding on an activity or a day out that they would all enjoy was pretty much impossible.

Honestly though, they may have been stroppy, grumpy, exhausting, full on, challenging, downright rude sometimes – all of those things and many more besides, but they were mine, my whole world, and even if I never got another full night's sleep ever again, I knew I wouldn't change any of them....... not for anything.

Littlest man had his first appointment with a consultant a couple of days before his birthday to discuss his numerous allergic reactions, we went in knowing he had a pretty severe egg allergy and came out diagnosed with cow's milk protein allergy (CMPA) and soya allergy, alongside possible allergies to aubergine and beetroot.

His new diagnosis explained all of the random contact reactions he had experienced where we hadn't been able to pinpoint egg as the cause, and also explained all of the symptoms he had ever had since birth, the eczema, "reflux" "hay fever" and "asthma" symptoms he had battled against were in fact all symptoms of CMPA and the fact that the medications provided for them had never truly worked was apparently typical.

The consultant congratulated me on continuing to breastfeed and suggested the best thing to do would be to carry on until he was 3 and able to have oat milk as his regular milk – he did say he would write to our GP and tell them to prescribe a specialist formula just in case we couldn't carry on but suggested that in fact that it tasted so disgusting that he probably wouldn't drink it anyway! Plus, as he had never actually taken a bottle anyway, we thought it was pretty pointless even trying.

So just in case we needed any motivation to carry on our breastfeeding journey (we really didn't – we were already aiming for the WHO recommendation of at least 2 years) we certainly had it now.

The plan was that he would be seen by a new consultant in 3 months' time, and they hoped to start some hospital-based testing when he was around 18 months old to see if we could reintroduce small amounts of milk/soya/egg into his diet. Until then I would be spending the next few weeks endlessly scouring packets for "safe" foods for him to eat and hoping that the elimination of these things from his diet would stop the reflux and asthma type symptoms and stop any more eczema flare ups, fingers crossed!

Soon enough, our smallest boy's 1st birthday arrived. It may sound terribly cliche, but it really had been the best year of my life, of course there had been highs and lows, but 99% of it had been happy, and having our family finally complete, watching our small army of little people growing up together had been truly amazing.

The way we had chosen to parent this time round had been completely different and making the parenting choices we had had changed me almost unrecognisably.

I had gained a confidence in myself and in my body that I never dreamed of having, it had changed my attitude towards others and their choices immensely, given me the courage to stand up for what was right for our children, to defend our decisions and choices as parents, and to give a voice to our children when they couldn't or wouldn't speak up for themselves.

Having smallest boy had made it even more obvious what an amazing daddy (and stepdad) my hubby was to all of our children, especially in the early days when I was sat feeding for hours on end despite him working 12-hour days he still came home and got everything done and played with the big kids.... and watching him with smallest boy melted my heart every single time.

Our live was far from perfect, but none of us ever claimed to be.... I still shouted and lost my temper too often, at least one of the big boys claimed they hated at least one of us every other day.... but seriously who's children don't?! But we all loved each other dearly, and every now and again they surprised us with just how lovely they could be – watching my biggest (HUGE, taller than me now) boy comforting his sobbing cousin recently made me realise despite the attitude he really was a lovely boy inside.

Our decision to have a large family and for me to stay at home meant that we didn't have spare cash for extravagant things, we didn't have a shiny new car (or in fact any car at all) and we wouldn't be going on any expensive holidays or days out anytime soon, in fact sometimes we had to turn down invitations to things or places because we just couldn't afford to go, but we neither wanted nor needed sympathy for that, we had made that decision and we would never regret it.

We had all that we needed, a roof over our heads, food on the table and more love than anyone could ever hope for.

For that reason, smallest boys' birthday wasn't an extravagant event, it was filled with the people he loved and his first taste of cake (egg and dairy free which was a new baking experience!) and we all had the most wonderful day.

THIRTY SEVEN

We had the loveliest family time over Christmas, we had all 4 of our children for a crazy morning of present opening, followed by 15 people round for dinner and laughter, all of the kids (and adults too) had been well and truly spoilt.

It was now New Year's Eve and over the past week we had eaten way too many desserts (thanks mum) been out for lunch, out for dessert, to the pantomime and to the cinema to watch Mary Poppins.

It's funny really, I'd never have even imagined taking a 12 month old to the pantomime or the cinema – I'd never have dared to take any of the big boys at that age, I'd have stayed at home whilst everyone else went for sure, but I didn't even think twice about taking smallest boy, we all went, him in the sling, and both times he fed and slept through the first half and cuddled up and half dozed/watched the second half – boobs have magical powers, I'm sure!

He absolutely loved the end of the pantomime and clapped, waved and danced as well as blowing kisses at the stage which was very cute! I was so glad for my increased confidence and that our parenting style this time round meant we really could take him anywhere at any time and he just happily fitted in to whatever we were doing and wherever we were going.

The past week had also seen smallest boys first shoes, and his first proper outside walk, as well as a new food allergy – tomatoes this time.

I had never been one for making New Year's resolutions – (mainly because I was rubbish at sticking to them) – so all I aimed to do this new year was to spend as much family time as possible and have as much fun and laughter as we could.

New Year's Eve was spent at home surrounded by family with lots of food, laughter, karaoke, fun and games – what more could we possibly wish for?!

The start of 2019 brought me a Velcro baby.... he was only happy when he was firmly attached to me. It was cold and miserable outside, the big boys were grumpy with their first full week back at school, me and smallest boy had had far too much of our own company – not that we didn't both love that, but it was pretty full on and I was missing actual conversation (as cute as a constant babababababa is of course).

I found myself wishing the days away until the spring when hopefully the weather would be a bit better, and we could get out and about more, but wishing the days away made me sad.... It felt like I had got everything we had wanted for so long and I should have been trying to enjoy every single day (or most of them at least) mum guilt was immense.

In all honesty despite us being a bit stir crazy at home and missing adult company (the highlight of our week other than the school run was a trip to Aldi!) I just didn't have the energy to deal with toddler groups and the constant chasing him round stopping him from eating every single piece of stray biscuit he could find, and/or smearing cake over himself and having a reaction. It was exhausting and just not fun for either of us, constantly taking things from him with him not understanding why he couldn't have them, so instead we just stayed at home.

So, roll on spring when we could spend our days on the park trying to eat grass and mud instead! It could not come soon enough, trips to the park had never seemed so appealing!

After another evening of ranting and moaning at my poor hubby about being stuck in the house staring at the same 4 boring walls all day every day, I suddenly had an idea... to stop moaning and instead do something about it – my solution however was probably not the obvious one...

The sensible way to solve the problem was probably to just woman up and get out more. Instead, I decided that if I hated looking at our boring beige living room so much then we should lose the beige...

By lunchtime the next day our old broken beige sofa was in pieces in the front garden awaiting the tip, by teatime I had convinced my sister and mum that we needed to go to ikea, and by midnight we had replaced the boring beige storage with rainbow colours, and ordered new cushion covers to match!

The next day we had new (well new to us at least) sofas and a new rug and I LOVED every single last bit of that room, now I couldn't wait to spend more time in it!

So maybe the solution to our problems wasn't always what we thought it might be... it's not always the obvious answer, it's about making the most of what we've got, in whatever way we can.

We may have had to borrow the kids Christmas money to pay for our new colourful things (it was January, seriously nobody has spare money in January, right?!) but sometimes we just needed to seize the moment, grab the idea and just go with it, do something drastic and make a difference.... and it really worked, our home was a happier place (and rest assured we paid them back on payday!)

A lovely friend said to me that week "you were probably feeling beige the past few years, and since smallest boy has come along, you're feeling colourful" and she couldn't have been more right.

Our lives seemed so much brighter in rainbow colours.

THIRTY EIGHT

I was slightly gobsmacked when smallest boy was 13 months old and someone asked me what he liked to watch on YouTube... he had never watched the TV never mind YouTube!

Maybe we were in the minority in not letting him have any "screen time" but I had read a lot about it recently and was very confident in our decision.

When we were at home during the day the tv was permanently switched off. We just didn't watch it at all. We had decided on no screen time until he was at least 2 and I have to say I was incredibly grateful he wasn't obsessed by some awful tv characters and their associated plastic tat (Iggle piggle was a firm favourite of both biggest boys at around this age and I could not subject myself to that again!!)

Anyway, he had a whole room full of books and beautiful wooden toys and was very happy to read and play all day long, we wanted that to continue for as long as possible before he became screen obsessed like his siblings!

I had just started a breastfeeding peer support course one evening a week so that I could volunteer to help breastfeeding mums and I loved it. One evening a week I got to be me, an actual adult, plus learn and meet other like-minded mums at the same time.

That had been the first of several big changes in the previous few weeks, we had also got an extra-large bed meaning there was finally enough space for all 3 of us which was amazing! Plus, we had begun to use cloth nappies.

I had met many cloth bum mummies since having smallest boy, and the thought of using them had always scared me, but they had been something I had wanted to try for a while, with only the initial cost stopping us.

But a lady at my WI was giving some away so I bit the bullet and got them, bought a few very cheaply on a local selling site and off we went. It was SO much easier than I anticipated, they worked perfectly, and they looked very cute too! Washing them was fine and seeing them all hanging on the washing line brought me far more joy than it probably should!

The cloth wipes smelt AMAZING and middle boy was thrilled that "we're saving the ocean" so all was good and smallest boys' eczema around his nappy was a million times better within days- a definite success.

I had been hearing so much about choices lately, school choices, diet choices, medical choices, relationship choices…. the list goes on and on, parenting choices are the ones that jumped out at me the most and seemed to be discussed so much on social media, they always seemed to spark massive debate and cause huge controversy!

I had lots of experience of different parenting choices, in fact at some point in my parenting journey I had tried a good many of them, but each and every choice that I had made as a parent had been the right one for me and my child in that moment.

Yes, time and experience had made me more confident in my choices, recently I had questioned some of the choices I made many years ago, but I didn't regret them, they had shaped my parenting journey, shaped my children into who they were, and I wouldn't change any of that for anything.

FEEDING choices are the spark of so many debates/discussions.... and they were choices I was particularly passionate about and choices I was constantly reading and seeking information about.

Bottle feeding, formula feeding, expressing breastmilk, breastfeeding .... I had done them all at some point along the way, and all had worked for me at some point.

I had expressed milk for my biggest boy whilst he was in neonatal intensive care, and only managed to breastfeed him twice, middle boy was given formula and a bottle from birth, and of course, smallest boy was very much a boob monster and had never taken a bottle or been given formula.

All of these choices had worked for my family in the moment, I have to say that feeding choices are the only ones I have any kind of regret about – the choices I question the most – I do wish I'd had the confidence to breastfeed when I was younger, and though I couldn't change the past I was hopeful that I could use my experiences to help others, to share knowledge and to boost their confidence in feeding choices. I couldn't wait to start my role as a peer supporter and share some of my experiences with other women.

SLEEP – the media was full of information about safe sleeping guidelines, the fact that me and hubby bed share with our smallest boy seemed to spark a lot of controversy, but once again, it is a decision that we had made that worked for us. (and yes, we did follow safe sleep guidelines – no one was more aware of them and paranoid about them than I was)

Bed sharing was not a choice I had made before, it wasn't possible with biggest boy because of the tubes and wires he had attached until he was 2.5 years old, however after that age he would regularly sleep with me at least for some of the night until he started school!

Middle boy never bedshared with us, not even once, he always preferred his own space, even when he was small, he would rather sleep in his buggy than with us, and as he got older even when he was poorly or upset and wanted to be close to us, he would sleep on the floor next to our bed rather than in with us.

Both big boys had their own bedrooms – biggest boy slept in his own room from being about 20 months, he slept through the night from being about 4 months old. Middle boy slept in his own room from about 6 months old but didn't sleep through the night until he was 2.5 years old.

Once again, different choices for different children, all choices that had worked for our family at the time.

We had no idea how long smallest boy would want to sleep alongside us? No idea how long he would still want to breastfeed several times throughout the night? What we did know though is that we would continue to do what worked for him and for us, regardless of anyone else's opinions.

PARENTING choices generally are such a minefield. This time round it was probably safe to say we were practising gentle parenting, attachment parenting – two terms I had never even heard of until smallest boy was born – but that now made so much sense to me and above all worked for us and our smallest boy.

They are parenting styles that were completely different to anything I had done before and are viewed by many as "crunchy" "alternative" or "hippy", but I was confident enough in myself to not be bothered by that, and to embrace it....in fact by this point I would bet my dungarees and tie-dyed t shirt along with my rainbow jumper that if those people read the gentle parenting books, they'd take something positive away from it!

Anyway, I digress…. my parenting choices were incredibly different this time around – but they worked for us. Just like the choices I made with the bigger boys worked for us at the time. I had no regrets.

I suppose what I'm trying to say is please try not to judge others by the choices they have made – I'm not saying I'm perfect – I'm far from it, I'm definitely guilty of judging people without knowing their background – but I'm making a conscious effort to think before I judge these days.

We often have no idea of the reasons behind people's choices. Parenting is tough enough without being judged by outsiders for every single thing you do or don't do.

Share the love, smile at fellow parents however they are feeding their babies, whether they are carrying their sleeping toddler or exhausted because they just won't sleep. Whether they've made the choice to stay at home or whether they've gone back to work…being a parent is hard whichever choices you make or indeed have made for you.

I was lucky to have an amazing hubby, fantastic family and a few wonderful friends to support my choices, alongside a group of amazing mummies at my LLL group who were parenting in similar ways to me this time around who provided no end of wisdom and support.

Not everyone is so fortunate.

As parents we should be holding each other up not tearing each other down.

THIRTY NINE

As Mother's Day approached again, I thought I would write my own version of "a Mother's Day" to distract myself and stop the stay at home mum guilt of "staying home doing nothing all day".

So, this is how my day looked:

- cuddled and reassured a sad 9-year-old at 1.30am after a nightmare

- kicked hubby out of bed when his alarm went off at 03.30

-fed and cuddled a sleepy poorly baby 3 times before anyone else woke for the day

- had the quickest shower in the world and got dressed at super speed whilst 9-year-old entertained smallest boy with a book

-made breakfast.... had breakfast thrown at me and all over the floor.... repeated many times until I gave up trying

-cleaned up the mess after breakfast

- refereed at least 3 arguments before 8am about who uses the bathroom first, who passes the toast to who, who left the milk/cereal/butter out etc

-somehow successfully got everyone dressed, fed, teeth brushed and out of the house to school

– carried a very unhappy small boy in the sling for pretty much 8 hours straight .... including a trip to the drs and to the shops and chemist

– given 9 syringes full of medicine – (nearly all successfully) and 10 puffs of inhaler

– bought and consumed chocolate after not having time for lunch

– thrown together a pasta bake and deposited in the oven whilst dancing with a crying baby in the sling

– searched the internet for baby iodine supplements after the previous day's hospital appointment informed me that he needed some .... in desperation order some seaweed to make sushi but eventually find a supplement and feel very grateful

– resort back to google to find a dairy free probiotic for a baby who is now on antibiotics in a desperate bid to avoid diarrhoea and extra nappy washing (google was my friend during nap time)

– remember middle boy wanted a parcel taking to school pick up; then also remember the toy dog I was left babysitting for the day by my 7-year-old niece and head to do the school run feeling like I'm winning at life.... (then realise I forgot snacks though my mum saved the day with enough to feed the 5000 and a trip to the ice cream van)

– collected a ridiculous number of children from school and took a trip to the park with friends

– walked the length of the park approximately a million times with grumpy baby in sling whilst everyone else played.... then be incredibly grateful when grumpy baby cheers up enough to go to play for 10 minutes to give my back a break

- sit on a park bench to feed and realise you're so tired you don't want to get back up again

- get home and feed 4 children tea, whilst throwing washing in the machine, reminding children to do homework, grabbing some food and preparing hubby some too

- patch up middle boys cut knee after his first attempt on his new Heelys

- take biggest boy to his basketball match and cheer him and his team on .... whilst texting hubby constantly checking on smallest poorly boy

- arrive home to house that looks like a rubbish dump.... ignore the mess and spend half an hour getting medicine into smallest boy and getting him to bed instead

- be very grateful that the 3 big kids are all in bed with no fuss for a change

- decide the house can wait, get into bed next to very wheezy baby and eat chocolate ice cream whilst frantically ordering food shopping to be delivered tomorrow so you don't all starve to death

- be very thankful we spent so much time attaching the cot to the bed so I can keep an extra close eye on smallest boy

- wonder why on earth I've spent 40 minutes writing this when I could've been asleep

– feed, cuddle, give inhalers.... repeat approximately hourly until the morning and then start all over again....

FORTY

By the time he was 18 months old he had had his worst allergic reaction yet, this time his mouth and tongue started to swell, but luckily a quick dose of his medication worked immediately and saved us a hospital trip.

We received smallest man's speech therapy referral, it was decided that his understanding was above the 2-year-old target, but his speech around 9-12 months. We weren't worried though, he was learning new signs very quickly and knew exactly how to communicate what he wanted to us!

He had also started spending 1 day a week with my mum and stepdad whilst I volunteered at the hospital doing breastfeeding peer support, which he loved!

He was growing in independence and character so incredibly quickly, learning and doing new things almost daily and watching him wrap his grandparents round his little finger was hilarious!

If anyone had told me I'd be breastfeeding my 18-month-old I'd have laughed a lot.... though if they'd said I'd be bedsharing with him, or that I'd be using cloth nappies or be a breastfeeding peer supporter that would've had the same reaction to be fair, yet here we were!

I am SO eternally grateful to the lovely friend who introduced me to my local LLL group in pregnancy after I told her I wanted to give breastfeeding a try, because I definitely wouldn't have got this far without her, and the amazing group of women I was so lucky to be a part of, they had encouraged and helped me in so many ways, not only in breastfeeding but in everything – our group WhatsApp was buzzing with so many different things it was fantastic.

Women supporting women, mothers supporting mothers, it was exactly how life should be.

That is exactly why I loved peer supporting so much, I was supporting other new mums to breastfeed, something I never even dreamed I would do, yet here I was, and I was loving every minute.

One Tuesday afternoon, just as I returned from my mornings volunteering, my auntie arrived to find me.

She had rushed around to tell me that my dad had just been found dead.

The next few days were a bit of a blur.

I went from trying to find out what had happened, to making funeral arrangements, cleaning up and clearing out his flat, whilst waiting for post-mortem results and dealing with a mountain of paperwork.

There was an awful lot of "adulting" done by me, from liaising with the coroner, to attending the register office, planning a funeral and writing a eulogy… most things being done on autopilot with no thought or time given to any emotion.

There wasn't much time to process things or think very much I was so busy with all the practical things.

I was asked so many times whether his death was "expected".

In all honesty I'm not sure anyone ever "expects" their parent to die. He wasn't "ill" as such, there was no time to say our goodbyes, one day he was there, going about life as usual, the next he was gone.

Yes, I knew his lifestyle wasn't exactly a healthy one, and he had had massive struggles with addiction for all of my adult life, but the last time I saw him he was full of life, I honestly wasn't expecting the next time I saw him to be in the chapel of rest.

Those who know me well will know of my relationship with my dad, I had always struggled to understand his way of life, always found his addiction difficult to understand, and I hated the way alcohol overtook everything and became the most important thing in his life.

I maintained a relationship with him despite all of this, despite it being incredibly difficult at times, seeing him weekly up until the big boys were smaller, doing his food shopping and collecting his prescriptions, and although I didn't see him as often in his last couple of years – every couple of months perhaps, he had made more of an effort since I was pregnant with smallest boy, phoning me almost weekly to check on me and him.

After his death I struggled with how to feel.

Grief is complex to begin with, but with a complex relationship added in it was mind blowing! I battled with myself about what was the right thing to do, and the right thing to feel, and felt very much like a hypocrite at times grieving for someone I could've made so much more effort with.

I felt shock, sadness and anger.

I cried and I laughed.

I felt guilty that I didn't see him on Father's Day, that the last communication I had with him was a quick text because I was too busy wrapped up in my own life to phone him.

Guilt that the last time I spoke to him I was mad with him, and I battled with myself to come up with the best things to do.

I was so incredibly grateful to my uncle for being there to help with all the practical stuff, and helping with all the decision making, I'm not sure what I'd have done without him in all honesty. It just goes to show how important family is.

My dad was far from perfect.

I'm the first to admit that I hated some of the choices he made. I hated the way he lived but despite all of his faults, and despite the far from perfect relationship we had, underneath there were many good memories too, especially without alcohol.

He was still my dad. I still loved him, and I would still miss him.

FORTY ONE

A few months passed by, with us trying to get on top of smallest boys' allergies. He got almost to the top of the soya ladder – (though we decided against introducing soya based alternative products as a regular part of his diet due to personal opinion) but despite that it did mean that the enormous amount of everyday foods that contain soya were now ok for him and he could share our bread at last!

He failed the milk ladder at the first step when he was accidentally given something, so that was put on hold for a while, and also failed the first step of the egg ladder - although we were expecting that due to the severity of his initial reaction to egg.

We had to wait another 3 months before we could try again so had a while to get his eczema back under control after his latest reactions.

Tomatoes were still out of his diet whilst we awaited some blood tests, but we made the decision that whilst we were managing his allergies perfectly fine that we didn't want to put him through any unnecessary trauma of blood tests and/or skin pricks unless absolutely necessary.

He suddenly started to talk too! Coming out with new words every day – and it was SO incredibly cute! Boobies being his favourite word!

"Are you STILL breastfeeding?!" seemed to be the number one question around that time...

And my answer was NO.

No, I was not STILL breastfeeding.

I was breastfeeding.

I was feeding my child in the normal, natural way, and believe it or not, contrary to societal norms he was not too old to do that.... the WHO recommends breastfeeding for 2 years AND BEYOND, we hadn't even reached their minimum recommendation yet, yet so many people seemed to think what we were doing was weird... so yes, we continued to breastfeed, whenever and wherever he would like to, to feed him, and to comfort him, and we would continue until one or both of us was ready to stop!

The other questions I answered a lot around this time....

Yes, he did sleep in our bed for at least half of every night.

Yes, he did have his own bed.

Yes, he did go in it most nights for a few hours.

Yes, he still breastfed throughout the night.

No, I don't care!

In fact, I cared so little that we bought a super king bed so that we all had enough space.... and it was AMAZING!

My response to anyone who thought my toddler should sleep in his own bed alone – I sleep alongside my husband every single night, as do so many others – if he's not there I struggle to sleep, we sleep beside our partners for comfort – why on earth would I expect my toddler not to require comfort and love in the night?!

Why would it be any different to during the day when he comes to me for love and cuddles?

Why in the middle of the night when everywhere is dark and quiet would I expect him to want to be alone?!

Our children are little for such a short space of time, they are solely dependent on us for such a short space of time in the grand scheme of things.... we would NEVER look back on this time and think we loved him or cuddled him too much!

For those people, whose opinion was that I was "making a rod for my own back" or that "he will be breastfeeding and sleeping in our bed til he's 18" well that's just that, their opinion, and of course they were entitled to it – but we were also entitled to ignore it - this was how we chose to parent, this is what worked for our family.

We chose to give our child the round the clock love and comfort that he craved – it is IMPOSSIBLE to spoil your child with love alone, and as a side note I'm pretty sure I've never met an 18-year-old who still breastfeeds and sleeps with their parents!

We were very aware that we were parenting very differently this time around – yes our older children were all sleeping in their own rooms by this point – though I hasten to add that actually our formula fed middle boy although he slept in his own bed in his own bedroom he actually still woke for milk in the night until he was 2.5 years old – and we (in all honesty actually 90% of the time it was daddy!) still went in and fed him and comforted him every single night .... so, it wasn't all that different!

I was lucky enough to have been introduced to and read so much about gentle parenting this time around, and to have met an army of amazing women who were all parenting in a similar way, which gave me the confidence to do what felt right.

We knew we were never going to get a chance to do this whole parenting thing again, that we would never get this time back. So, we were doing what we believed was right for our child, for our family, in each moment, with the knowledge and skills that we had.

If that meant that I was referred to as a crunchy, hippy mum sat on the grass feeding her toddler whilst other people stared and judged then I was ok with that.

In fact, I was more than happy with that. I loved our way of life, our way of parenting, our little family.

FORTY TWO

One day when he was 21 months, I went to check on smallest boy who was sleeping upstairs and noticed he was breathing very quickly and wheezing quite badly.

He had been fine just half an hour earlier when he went for his nap, although had had a bit of a cold for a couple of days. He became worse quite quickly and I managed to get an emergency drs appointment for a couple of hours later.

The Dr saw us and prescribed him some antibiotics, said he had a chest infection and that he was on the borderline of needing to go to hospital but to give him a double dose of antibiotics when we got home and hopefully, he would improve.

2 hours later we were getting him ready for bed when his breathing suddenly got worse again, we rang 111 and within 5 minutes, in less time than it took Grandad to walk round the block to collect the big boys, we saw blue lights and heard the siren of an ambulance at the front door.

Within seconds he was being given oxygen and then a nebuliser and we were whisked straight into hospital. I think in that couple of hours I aged several years.

He was admitted to the children's ward where he needed oxygen all night and was needing 10 puffs of inhaler every 4 hours which he didn't like at all.

Luckily every single member of NHS staff we saw were amazing, from the lovely paramedic who couldn't have been nicer, who when he realised he was breastfed, told me how his wife had fed their daughter until she was 4 and suggested I fed him throughout all of his treatment to keep him calm – which worked amazingly, to the lovely nurse who when I explained he didn't sleep in a cot because we bedshared went and got a single bed with sides on so that we could sleep together.

We were discharged after he could sleep without needing any oxygen, and he could tolerate 8 puffs of inhaler every 4 hours and left in the care of the community nurses with open access to go back to the ward if we needed to.

Fast forward a few days and he was a million times better, he had got his smile back, and I felt less like the walking dead. It took a while to wean him down from his inhalers and to start eating again and although he couldn't do very much at all without getting out of breath for a few days he could soon talk again and quickly got back to his cheeky self!

Parenting isn't always easy, in fact at times it's really bloody hard, exhausting, emotional and scary.

Watching your toddler really struggling to breathe is hard – even when you've been there so many times with his biggest brother, you're never prepared for it.

You're never immune to how traumatic it is watching a paramedic or a nurse fighting to help your child when you can't help them yourself.

Watching your child so upset and not understanding why they can't move from the bed, or why they have to wear the oxygen mask, or have the wires attached to them is so hard. Doing everything you can possibly think of to help them and it still not being enough is heart-breaking.

Only 3 weeks later we were in an almost identical scenario, a slight sniffle one day, full on wheezing, struggling to breathe and requiring nebulisers and oxygen the next day.... a 3 day stay in hospital this time and once again discharged into the care of community nurses to try and wean him down from inhalers.

We were all exhausted and emotionally drained. The bigger boys had been shipped off to family and missed us a lot, middle boy was a little traumatised by the ambulance, but smallest boy once again bounced back very quickly, and we hoped that was the last of it.

Sadly, we were very wrong. Only a couple of weeks passed before once again his wheezing resulted in an early morning trip to A&E, they immediately realised he had no air entry into one lung, and he was quickly whisked for a chest x-ray and another stay on the children's ward.

This time the diagnosis was pneumonia, we were eventually discharged home, with more community nurse visits, and lots of inhalers and antibiotics and despite every nurse and junior doctor we saw saying he needed a diagnosis the registrar STILL said they couldn't diagnose asthma until he was 2 so we were no closer to getting anyone to make a diagnosis or prescribe him any preventative medication. Suffice to say I was exhausted, he was going a bit stir crazy, and it seemed to be taking longer and longer to wean him off his inhalers.

After his 4th wheezy hospital admission within 10 weeks, we were all just a little bit tired and fed up with the constant illness and battle to keep him well.

The big kids seemed relatively unphased by the number of times they had been shipped off to someone's house at a moment's notice and had found their own new normal, and whilst we were very thankful to everyone who had taken them in/helped with school runs and ran around after us, we had had enough!

Smallest boy had developed a new obsession with ambulances – it seemed he had enjoyed the blue lights far more than mummy did and was the proud owner of his very own doctors kit and wooden ambulance and was found most often making siren noises whilst whizzing around the floor!

On a positive note, after being told for months that they couldn't make a diagnosis or offer any preventative treatment until he was 2 the consultant did see him at his poorliest on his 4th admission and he didn't think twice about prescribing him a preventative medication at last! His words were "somebody needs to stand up and do something about this, so I'll be the one to do it".

It was 11pm and we'd been there all day, I had lost all hope by that point and when he said it, I honestly could've kissed him!! So, finally we had slightly more hope that he would stay out of hospital for a little longer this time (the previous time we managed a grand total of 12 days - being back in only 6 days after finishing his last course of antibiotics for pneumonia).

Despite all of his illnesses and hospital stays it hadn't all been doom and gloom, after over a year of not attending any kind of toddler groups etc as it was so difficult to stop him from finding other people's snacks and me deciding it just wasn't worth the stress, we found a group that didn't involve any kind of food or snack time and that he loved! (The downside being that he kept having to miss it as he was too poorly to go).

FORTY THREE

With every cliche there ever was, time really flew by and before we knew it, it was the day before smallest boy's 2nd birthday.

I took my moment to be nostalgic and reminisce.

It hadn't all been easy of course, but every last second, every sleepless night (and yes, they were still frequent – and no I didn't want any advice on how to make them stop thanks!) every smile, every memory, it had all been worth it.

I was the happiest I had ever been.

I reckon I had probably aged 20 years in the past 2 years, our smallest boy had certainly kept us on our toes, but he had brought so much joy into so many people's lives, especially mine.

2 years earlier I had been sat at home, bags packed, excited for the next day, but terrified at the same time. Hoping and praying that we would get to bring home a healthy baby, after a really tough pregnancy.

A lovely friend (who is now smallest boy's fairy godmother) had taken me along to an LLL meeting earlier that day, where I had met some lovely ladies, and confirmed that yes, I could breastfeed my baby immediately after having a caesarean, despite having gestational diabetes, and that I didn't need to let anybody give him formula.

I remember saying to hubby that I was confident I would meet my goal of exclusively breastfeeding for at least 2 weeks, until he went back to work.

I would never in a million years have thought that 2 years later I would be about to feed a 1-year-old for the last time, that when I got up the next morning (or who am I kidding – probably 1am…and 4am….and another 20 times throughout the night!) I would be feeding a 2-year-old…. I know there's no way on earth I anticipated feeding for this long, but I was SO incredibly happy and grateful that I had been able to.

It's no secret how different our parenting journey had been this time around. I used to find it funny when people referred to us as "hippy" or "crunchy" for breastfeeding past infancy, for baby wearing, cloth nappying, bed sharing, the lack of plastic crappy toys and using gentle parenting approaches…. I didn't find it funny anymore, I took it as a compliment.

I had learnt so much from an assortment of women during the past 2 years, and we had muddled our way through to a parenting style that fitted and worked for our family, and we were all so much happier for it.

We were raising a happy, confident, boy with an amazing attachment, and an ever-changing personality. We had a house filled with open ended, eco-friendly, ethical and sustainable toys, that all of our children could play with together. We had no guilt about plastic, or any need for 100 batteries, no annoying music, or headache inducing flashing lights.

The no screen rule we had for smallest boy meant he wasn't begging for the latest tv character plastic tat, (because he didn't even know who they were!)

Not only were we saving our sanity, but we also didn't have to endure hours of mindless rubbish on tv, we were saving money, and the planet…. and of course, the real reason we had no screen time – hopefully, his brain development was as good as it possibly could be, and his imagination was used at every opportunity... he learnt so much through play, and through watching others.

I was so incredibly proud to have reached 2 of my biggest parenting goals - to breastfeed to meet the WHO target of 2 years and beyond - not one single drop of formula had ever passed his lips, (which I think is the biggest achievement I have ever had!) and also to also meet their target of no screen time before the age of 2 (despite a couple of documentaries on a very long car journey down south!) and we had no plans on changing either of those things anytime soon.

In fact, natural term weaning was now my goal, I had learnt so much about the benefits of breastfeeding beyond infancy and had seen first-hand how vital breast milk can be in toddlerhood. My initial goal of 2 weeks, which eventually stretched to 6 months, then to 1 year seemed like so long ago!

Breastfeeding was now my favourite parenting tool.

hungry – boob

thirsty- boob

fallen over – boob

tired- boob

upset – boob

You get the idea!

It was about so much more than nutrition, it brought him comfort and connection, it sent him to sleep, it allowed us that time together to build attachment and strengthen our bond.

The me of 2 years earlier would not believe the confidence I had found in myself, I had fed him absolutely everywhere, in front of anyone, just that day he had fed to sleep in our local theatre!

I still sometimes even 2 years down the line struggled to believe that we really did have everything we ever wanted. After 3 and a half years of infertility and then multiple miscarriages, that our little rainbow baby had brought us so much love and happiness.

Even now I sometimes had to take a moment to realise just how far we had come.

Smallest boy had a lovely birthday, he really wasn't impressed by presents, he didn't want to open them, or want anyone else to either! Although when we did eventually manage to, he was very excited by all his new toys and clothes!

We had a lovely few days, hubby had 5 days off work, and we managed a couple of days out just the 3 of us whilst the big kids were at school, then a fab big family trip out at the weekend for his birthday treat and a trip to see Santa – who he liked from afar but was definitely not a fan of up close!!

The week that followed was a busy one, with a trip to the dentist, his 2nd chickenpox vaccination – which wasn't quite as easy as the first as he remembered as soon as we walked into the room and didn't want his trousers pulling down – it also involved a slightly awkward conversation with the pharmacist who was asking him whether he wanted a paw patrol or SpongeBob plaster and was actually open mouthed when I explained he didn't watch tv so didn't know who either of them were – she still insisted on trying to put one on him though – and he promptly screamed at her, hit it out of her hand and said no …. I'm not sure how I didn't laugh!

Next was his 2-year development check, which went fantastically, there were no longer any concerns about his speech, she didn't judge our decision to bedshare, and the only downside was a referral to podiatry about his gait – he was taking after his big brother there!

The next appointment of the week was with his consultant. This was AMAZING. She could not have been any nicer. We now finally had a much better plan regarding his asthma/hospital admissions/medications, and she could not praise us enough for continuing to breastfeed through his allergies and illnesses, and for parenting the way we did. I left with a renewed confidence in our NHS and our local hospital.

Our final appointment was straight after this, for him to have some blood tests. He was super brave, the nurses were amazing with him and despite a little whimper when the needle went in, he sat and watched fascinated by the blood coming out, it was only after they'd done that he got upset as his hand was bleeding and he didn't like the pressure the nurse had to keep applying – it bled for quite a while and she had to keep increasing pressure which he hated, but he was an absolute superstar and despite ripping off the plaster (a bit of a theme here I think) he was very happy to get a sticker and go home!

It was finally the Christmas holidays, and the bigger kids were super excited.

Christmas wasn't my favourite time of year, and this year was no different.

Every year for the past 14 years there had been someone missing at Christmas.

Every year I had visited the cemetery with gifts for my first-born child.

Every year I had wondered what would have been on her Christmas list, what she would have been opening on Christmas morning.

Every year I had shed a tear for what should have been.

For the first few years I would always go to the cemetery on Christmas Day, but now the boys were bigger they understandably didn't like to go, so we went on Christmas Eve instead, we decorated with Christmas ornaments and took cards, because that's all we could do.

I'm not writing this for sympathy, I'm writing it because it's real…. it is the reality for so many bereaved parents and so many of them are forgotten about at this time of year, so many of them don't have a voice, a platform to be heard, so many don't have the opportunity to speak about their child, their loss, their grief, and that makes me sad.

I'm also writing it to show that although my pain is still there, and I do still cry every single year that I spend Christmas without my baby girl, that it does get easier, that although that sadness will always be there, that she will always be missing, although Christmas like many other occasions will always be tinged with sadness, now, all these years later I could smile and enjoy this time of year.

Yes, it was nowhere near as difficult as that very first Christmas was anymore. That first year, I watched my niece open her presents and then went back to bed for hours to avoid all the fun I should've been having.

As the years had passed and our family had grown it had become much easier, it was easy to get distracted by the excited children, the ridiculous amount of presents and the smiles and laughter. In fact, I'd go as far as to say I actually enjoyed

Christmas these days, but occasionally I was still caught off guard.

This year there were another 2 people missing from my life, my dad and my second mother, my mum's best friend. We had lost her to cancer in the summer and missed her so much.

Since I became a parent, she had my back in so many ways – we shared so many laughs about bringing up boys, and she had always been there through every single thing.

Who was going to get me through the teenage years now?!

When I went to see her in hospital just a couple of weeks before she died, despite being incredibly poorly, she told me how proud she was of me for how much I had achieved since having smallest boy.

Her last words to me when I went to say goodbye will stay with me forever – even struggling to breathe she still managed to make me laugh!

I had felt both hers and my dad's losses often in the run up to Christmas. We had had some photos of the kids taken a few weeks earlier and I couldn't figure out how I'd ended up ordering too many.... until I realised, I was so used to sending them to my dad and auntie in their Christmas cards.

My Christmas food shop was half its size because I wouldn't be delivering a hamper to my dad on Christmas Eve.

I had bought and wrapped presents for our children from my auntie every year for as long as I could remember to save her the stress – who was I supposed to wind up about being organised now?!

There was no one moaning at me constantly to make her favourite Malteser cake, and who the bloody hell was gonna cook the turkey? Turn up on Christmas Day in their slippers? Eat too much, nip home "for a trump" and then reappear an hour later for pudding and get fizzy?! Who was going to sing karaoke all night on New Year's Eve?

There was going to be a big gap at our dinner table that Christmas (and probably lots of food left too!)

Thank goodness for all of our wonderful memories.

The point to my rambling here is to be mindful of all of the people who are missing someone on special occasions, whether that be a religious festival, a birthday or a holiday, whether they are missing a child or an adult, whether it's a grief that's new and raw or a loss that happened decades ago, it still hurts.

Let people know that you're thinking of them, they will appreciate it, I'm sure. And if you're lucky enough to spend Christmas with all of your children/family then count your blessings, you are one of the lucky ones.

Enjoy it, don't stress about the small things, hold them a little closer, hug them a little tighter, and play with them a little longer. You only get this time once, make memories that both you and they will keep forever.

That Christmas and new year passed in a bit of a whirlwind of love and laughter. And soon enough we realised we had got to the end of a decade, and what a decade that had been!

10 years earlier, I had moved to live back home with my mum, with a 3-year-old biggest boy and was 7 months into a hellish

pregnancy with my middle boy...how my life had changed since then.

In 2010 I had my middle boy and moved out of my mum's house as a single parent with my 2 boys. shortly afterwards I got together with my amazing hubby, and later that year we started a very lengthy court battle.

10 years down the line that was all a distant memory, 8 years ago, we had got engaged, and our journey to extend our family had begun.

We had lost a few people along the way, some important people in our lives had passed away, and others had walked away.... but we entered a new decade with no regrets.

With the knowledge that we had been, and would continue to be, the best parents we could for all of our children, and that we would support each other and love each other no matter what.

EPILOGUE

1 in 4.... just take a moment to think about that.

For every 4 women you know the odds are at least 1 of them has dealt with some form of baby loss, whether that be miscarriage, stillbirth or neonatal death.

That is a LOT of women.

Yet still no one is talking about it.

Well, no one except me and a seemingly small number of others who have been through the utter devastation that comes alongside the experience.

SO many women are still suffering in silence.

Some may think I over share, but I will keep on telling my own personal story until I'm no longer capable of doing, because if it helps just ONE person feel less alone in their own experience then it is worth it.

I have retold the stories of both of my miscarriages in graphic detail, buy why?

Because before I experienced it, I had no idea. No clue about the physical pain, and no clue about how truly awful it would be.

I had NO IDEA that I'd have to undergo surgery, NO IDEA I'd have contractions and labour pains and NO IDEA how much it would affect me emotionally.

There's this unwritten rule that you don't tell anyone about a pregnancy until you're past the magic 12 weeks.... meaning that hundreds of women are struggling through this ALONE like it is no big deal....

It is a HUGE deal when you're in the midst of it.

It is hell.

Women NEED support. Women NEED other women to tell their own stories, and men do too.

We underestimate the effect these things have on them.

They were their babies too.

They were just as excited; they are grieving too. although mums are often given "a few days off to recover" the dads are often forced to remain as normal and pretend nothing at all has happened.

This taboo needs to end.

And if me oversharing my own experiences helps one tiny bit then I won't apologise for keep doing so.

Baby loss.... it's been 16 years since my own experience of neonatal death, and I'm happy to say that care and support has improved massively in this area in those years. But there is still so much more that could be done.

That raw grief left me some time ago. I can't honestly remember when, but somehow it did, and I carried on.

There were days I didn't want to.... but not anymore.

These days the tears are rare, these days the most common feeling is guilt, guilt that I haven't thought about her today, or this week even, guilt that her garden at the cemetery probably needs weeding and these days I just don't go as often as I used to.... guilt that I've somehow replaced her with her brothers, that I've somehow moved on and left her behind.

Of course, none of that is true. None of it makes sense rationally. She will always be a piece of me, a missing piece of course, but my love for her is ingrained in me.

I am still her mummy, and always will be.

On her 14th birthday I attended a birthday party for one of smallest boys' little friends. In any previous year there's no way I'd have even contemplated that. In fact, I'd have run a million miles in the past. But I was stronger. Stronger than I had ever been, and I had realised that continuing with life as normal did not make me a bad person, or a bad mother.

There are no clear right or wrong answers when parenting, and that includes parenting a child who isn't here with you.

Whatever you do you feel guilt. Guilt for carrying on as normal, guilt for not carrying on as normal. Guilt for being happy, guilt for being sad.... the list goes on.

Grief is a journey, just like parenting. And whatever you feel in any given moment is ok. Whatever you do, whatever decision you make in any given moment is ok, as long as it feels right for you and your child.

The majority of parents need to learn to be kinder to themselves, whether they are new parents or many years down the line, whether their children are still with them or not.

Parenting in any situation is tough, and we don't give ourselves enough credit for the things we get right, focusing far too often on the things we get wrong.

However much your children or loved ones drive you mad.... hold them a little closer, hug them a little tighter, and give them a little more of your time.... I know I wish I could.

Nobody ever looks back and regrets spending too much time with the ones they love.

I don't struggle with my grief anymore. 99% of the time I can think of my beautiful girl with a smile. I am thankful that I am her mummy and for all the things that having her, and her death have taught me. For the friends I have made along the way, and for the way in which I have changed because of her.

That's not to say I don't miss her. I always will.

I will always wonder who she would've been.

There will always be moments that take my breath away when something reminds me of her.

STILL 16 years after her death I struggle to find the right answer when somebody I've just met asks me the most dreaded question:

"how many children have you got?"

It's something I've talked about time and time again with a couple of friends in similar circumstances, and you'd think by now I'd have the perfect answer, but in all honesty, it still catches me off guard most of the time.

In certain situations – medical appointments etc it's easy to just be matter of fact, no questions asked, but sometimes it's much harder to find the right response, especially when you're on the spot.

There are 3 options really:

Tell the truth…. he is my 4th child, then go on to explain that his big sister died…. leaving myself open for either awkward silence or future avoidance.

Or, say I have 3 boys…. also, the truth… but this way I get to breathe a sigh of relief that I don't get the sympathetic comments or awkward silence and just carry on as normal.

The problem with the second option is that I then feel guilty for the rest of the day for not including my beautiful girl…and should I happen to speak to that person again then they don't know the whole truth about my family.

The third option is my default these days – I have 4. At this point I usually pray that the conversation stops there, but if not, I can either say, I have 3 boys and a step daughter – true. Or I can tell them about my baby girl.

There is no easy option really, and whichever one I choose I can't really win and will feel guilty.

Life isn't always easy…. I may be stronger, more confident and happier than I've ever been, that is all true…. but underneath everything else I'm human and can be caught off guard now and then.

There will always be moments that catch me unaware.

I sometimes watch my eldest niece (who was born only 2 months after my daughter) doing something for the first time, and feel sad for what should have been, sometimes one of my boys will say something or ask something about their sister, or one of my nieces will say something matter of fact about her being "dead" and these days it almost always makes me smile.

I love that they all include her in their family, love that they talk so openly and honestly about her – even though of course I wish they didn't have to, that she was there causing trouble alongside them instead, but somehow them all talking about her brings comfort that she'll never be forgotten.

What I must say is that there's no "right way" to grieve, something I've learnt over the past 16 years, it really is unpredictable, an indescribable journey that you just have to navigate your way through the very best you can... it's unique to every single baby loss parent, although some people's journeys are similar no two can ever be the same, because everybody's story is different, everybody's grief is different.

If you've read this far thankyou.... please don't be disheartened, if someone you know or love has been through, or goes through baby loss in the future, please don't say nothing for fear of making them sad.

Please don't cross the road or walk the other way, sometimes just being there is enough.

If they are happy to talk, ask them about their baby, use their babies name, ask them who their baby looked like, ask them all of the questions you would ask a parent with a living child, how was their labour/birth? How much did baby weigh?

Please don't think that by mentioning their baby you will make them sad – they are already as sad as they could possibly be.

Let them know that you're thinking of them, don't be a stranger.... personally, I have no friends left from before I lost my daughter. A couple of friendships did survive for a while, and I'll always be grateful to those who came to visit me (and to the one friend who came to the hospital and asked if she could hold my baby) and to those who came to show their support at her funeral, but I neither see nor speak to any of those people anymore.

I am a different person to who I once was, and life moves on much differently for someone who has experienced such loss.

Be there for that friend or family member, be patient, keep inviting them out, keep texting, keep sending cards, one day they will be ready to reply and face the world again.

I've spoken a little about healing, and since the arrival of our smallest boy and the completion of our big crazy family I really do feel like I've done a lot of healing, I no longer struggle with seeing new babies, even up until our smallest boy was born the thought of holding a baby girl made me feel physically sick, I'd do almost anything to avoid it.... but that is definitely not the case anymore.

I'll always be her mummy, she'll always be my baby girl, and I'll always miss her, as long as I live, I'll wonder who she would have been, but through all the sadness, the grief and the utter heartbreak, one important fact remains....

Once upon a time I held the most beautiful baby girl in my arms, I'd fought so hard to keep her alive, and we made it, albeit only briefly, but in those few short minutes I got to tell her how loved she was, in those few precious moments I became a mummy.

In her very short life, she taught me so much about myself, and about being a mummy, and without her knowing she helped shape me into the person I am today. Despite all the pain, and how much I wish things had ended differently, I'll always be grateful that I am her mummy, and for anyone just beginning this horrible journey, its shit, really shit.... but I promise it DOES get easier.

My life is no longer defined by my loss and my grief.

I will always make my story heard, tirelessly fight for greater awareness and greater support for those who are going through similar experiences in the hope that one day people will suffer much less. That one-day baby loss will be less of a taboo, that people will be able to grieve and be honest about their experiences and their feelings.

Baby loss awareness week is a great time to spread awareness, to share stories and photos and make every voice heard.

Every single life matters.

Every single pregnancy matters. No matter how long or short.

We love them from the very first moment that blue line appears, and we will love them until our last breath.

There is nothing better, yet nothing harder, than becoming a parent.

Losing a child is the closest to hell any of us will ever experience.

Let's hold each other up, listen to those who need it, and share our experiences in the hope they will make a difference to somebody else.

To my smallest and last boy, you have taught me so much in such a short time, and as cliched as it sounds, I really have loved every moment, there have been tough days, and times when sleep deprivation has reduced me to tears, but it's been an amazing journey so far and I truly am excited to see where we go from here.

A part of me is sad that it's going so fast, that I'll never be doing any of this ever again, that every time you hit a new milestone that you're growing up and needing me less and less, but the rational part of me loves it, watching you grow and learn new skills almost daily makes me so proud.

Being your mummy has been such a new experience for me, everything we're doing is so different to how I've ever parented before, and as much as I love it, I sometimes feel sad that I didn't have the knowledge and confidence to parent this way with your brothers.

Although you are my 4th child we're definitely learning as we go along, and I'm learning so much about myself, and gaining confidence and finding my voice more and more each day, being your mummy has given me confidence and turned my views and life around completely, so thankyou smallest boy.

To my middle boy, I may have raised you differently to how I am raising your little brother, but I did it the only way I knew how, I did exactly what I thought was right for you, what was right for all of us at the time, and although with hindsight there are so many things I could have done differently, what I did worked!! Look at you now, you are about to transition to high school, to start a whole new chapter of your own.

You have grown into the most incredible, loving, son and brother and although you drive me completely and utterly crazy, you make me proud beyond belief. Seeing the young man, you've grown into is amazing, and watching you play or read with your little brother makes my heart melt every single time .... so, thank you for being incredible.

To my biggest boy, you may not have been my first child, your beautiful sister took that title, I may not have been a first-time mum when you came quietly into my life 15 years ago, but you were my first time at parenting, and wow what a learning curve that has been!

It's hard to believe the teenage boy in front of me, now taller than me, in fact started out in life so quietly, so fragile, that your life hung in the balance so precariously for so long. those first weeks in intensive care, those first years requiring oxygen and daily nurse visits, so many times we nearly lost you, so many times you fought so hard to stay.

I want to go back to those drs today and shout and scream at them, "look.... look at this huge, amazing young man.... he's the one you told me would never survive.... he's the one you said would die.... would be blind or deaf, wouldn't meet any of his milestones.... just you look at him now!!"

I could not be prouder of the young man you are today. Don't get me wrong you are far from perfect! you drive me crazy almost every day but you're always the one to come and ask for a hug, I hope that never stops.

You're almost ready for your last year at school, and you have achieved so much, watching you do what you love and enjoy life so much makes my heart happy.

To my baby girl, I will always wonder who you would have been.

You taught me more about love, life and myself in those few short minutes of your life than anybody else had ever taught me, or ever has since.

Although there are things, I wish I'd done differently for you, or with you, (I have spent many many hours, days even reliving some of the decisions I made in those first few hours and days after you were born) I have learnt not to torture myself with those thoughts.

I will miss you eternally, torturing myself with what ifs will not change that.

You were, and always will be, the most beautiful girl I have ever seen, and those precious few minutes I was lucky enough to spend with you in my arms before you were gone will forever be both the most amazing, most cherished, yet also the most painful of my life.

To follow more of our journey feel free to follow:

http://motherhoodthejourneyblog.wordpress.com

Facebook page:

Motherhoodthejourney – blog

Instagram:

Motherhoodthejourney

Printed in Great Britain
by Amazon